Teaching Phonics in the
Literature-Based Classroom

Teaching Phonics in the Literature-Based Classroom

Dorothy Fowler

and

Jean Frey

Christopher-Gordon Publishers, Inc.
Norwood, Massachusetts

Credits

Every effort has been made to contact copyright holders for permission to reproduce borrowed material where necessary. We apologize for any oversights and would be happy to rectify them in future printings.

Christopher-Gordon Publishers, Inc.
1502 Providence Highway
Norwood, Massachusetts
(800) 934-8322

Printed in the United States of America

10 9 8 7 6 5 4 3 2 1   03 02 01 00

ISBN: 1-929024-19-3
Library of Congress Catalogue Number: 00-102377

DEDICATION

To Larry

for being there

—J.F.

To Michelle

for helping me see life's possibilities

and

To Lew

for helping me make the possibilities realities

—D. F

Contents

✷ ACKNOWLEDGMENTS ✷

This book began with a belief about quality practices related to the teaching of phonemic awareness and phonics. We are grateful to Ann McCallum for believing that we might be able to convey that belief to others and for helping to make that belief a reality. Ann is our mentor, our inspiration, and our friend.

We are very indebted to the extraordinary teachers with whom it has been our privilege to work as we wrote the book. They invited us into their classrooms and shared not only their teaching practices but also their students and the work that their students produced. The teaching practices that are so basic to their classrooms are the quality practices that we hope will become part of every child's school experience. Time spent observing the teaching and learning experiences in their classrooms is the very best professional development experience. We hope that we have captured these practices with enough clarity for our audience to sense the wonder of watching these young learners as they become literate individuals. In particular, we would like to thank Nanci Kurtz, Emelie Parker, Heather Norton, Melissa Fleisher, Christie Sens, Carrie Cayton, Sabrina Shea, and Margarette Peterson.

We also wish to thank Bill Harp for giving us the opportunity to produce this work and for his support and guidance as the work became a reality. His patience and understanding was always welcome and much appreciated. Finally, we wish to express our appreciation to the reviewers of the manuscript. Their reflective and thoughtful comments were extraordinarily helpful in bringing clarity to the work.

PREFACE

We embarked on the challenge of writing a book about teaching phonics because we believe that teachers need a voice in the dialogue on teaching phonics. We emphasize that it is not a matter of *whether* phonics should be taught but *how*. All readers and would-be readers need to have a knowledge of phonemic awareness and phonics; it is critical to successful reading. However, we do not want to see the instruction of phonics return to isolated drills and work sheets unrelated to reading that engages, enchants, and informs. To this end, we have written *Teaching Phonics in the Literature-Based Classroom*. It is our hope that this volume contributes to teachers' repertoire of reading techniques and strategies while reinforcing their background in the theory that informs their practices.

In chapter 1 we begin with an overview of research on phonics instruction. At the same time we provide vignettes of classroom teachers and children engaged in teaching and learning about phonics. We discuss the reading process and the challenge of teaching beginning readers to use all sources of information. We set the scene for both phonics instruction and the rest of the book.

Chapter 2 provides descriptions of what phonics instruction looks like in literature-based classrooms. Again we provide vignettes at different instructional levels. We also want the reader to understand the environment, management, and materials that are needed to effectively develop readers who use all the resources available in print. It has been our experience that sometimes the management of books and children has presented a bigger challenge to teachers than knowing what to teach.

Chapters 3 and 4 present definitions and descriptions of the differences between phonological awareness and phonemic awareness. We describe how children can be supported in the development of phonological and phonemic awareness through language play. Children love rhymes, chants, songs, and finger plays. As children become aware of language, their ability to identify and manipulate phonemes develops with time, experience, and instruction. We offer ways to teach and assess the development of both phonological and phonemic awareness.

Teaching the alphabet is the topic of chapter 5. We recognize that children must have knowledge of the alphabet to read and write effectively. We offer a discussion of ways to instruct children in the alphabet while delighting in books. We include a thorough description of different kinds of alphabet books that meet different instructional needs.

In chapter 6 we define phonics and launch into a complete discussion of instructional and assessment methods. We describe instruction and lessons at different grades conducted by successful teachers we have worked with and observed. Assessment of students' knowledge and use of phonics is critical to the instructional decisions a teacher makes. We show how teachers assess and make decisions about how to best teach children based on those assessments. Samples of student assessments and teacher decisions are supplied.

Chapter 7 discusses developing word recognition skills and strategies. Automaticity and sight words are defined and discussed. We offer a number of ways to increase students' awareness of words, word patterns, and word parts. A number of activities and games for helping students to apply their knowledge of letters, sounds, and words are provided. Using books to develop word recognition is also described. A critical element to effective reading is vocabulary development. We provide research linking reading quantity with vocabulary development.

Finally, chapter 8 furnishes a discussion of the structural analysis of words and how to teach it. The importance of knowing how to apply knowledge of structural analysis is provided. We also offer a collection of games and other activities that will help students to use their knowledge of structural analysis to problem solve words during both reading and writing.

Throughout the book, we provide classroom examples of students learning how to apply phonics to reading. Each chapter discusses how to assess the children's skill and progress in using phonics.

The appendixes provide a list of alphabet books and books especially useful for developing phonemic awareness.

We have written this book with the teachers of all young children in mind, it can therefore be a useful tool for teachers in preschool, kindergarten, and the primary grades. Research continues to support the view that phonological awareness begins to develop in children as young as 3 years old. The ideas in this book can support preschool teachers as they plan language and literacy experiences that develop phonological awareness. The information and learning experiences discussed in the book will support children as they move through the development of phonological awareness, from awareness of rhyme to manipulation of individual phonemes. The book will also be of value to student teachers, teacher educators, and teachers working in remedial reading programs; it will answer your questions about phonics, provide you with a vocabulary to discuss phonics instruction, and most important, offer you sound instructional and assessment methods. We hope you teach all aspects of reading, including phonics, using literature that will entice your students to become successful lifelong readers.

CHAPTER 1

 Setting the Scene ✳

Every year on the Tuesday after Labor Day, there is a moment when I look out at the group of first graders assembled in front of me for the first time and a feeling of anxiety comes over me. I am so awed by the responsibility of helping these children become readers, that I am momentarily breathless. Then, one by one, I notice the enthusiasm, energy, and expectation in their faces and the moment is gone and I know that each one of them will learn to read. It is their enormous potential that challenges me and demands that I become the teacher they need. As I have come to understand reading and readers better, I have changed the techniques and strategies I have used for reading instruction. However, consistently, there has been a need for phonics instruction.

—Dorothy Fowler

Phonics remains a hot topic in education, and it will always be a significant part of the conversation when reading is discussed. Historically, debate on the role of phonics in learning to read has persisted over decades. Literature on the methods used for teaching reading shows that phonics as the main instructional focus for beginning readers has moved in and out of vogue (Strickland, 1998). Two points are worth noting when looking at methods used for teaching reading. The first is that no single method of reading instruction has been superior to others for all children, perhaps because reading is a complex activity and children bring such varied experiences and backgrounds to the task of learning to read (Bond & Dykstra, 1967, 1997). The second is that phonics plays a role in instruction regardless of the approach chosen for teaching reading. Readers must come to understand the relationship between letters and sounds if they wish to move beyond beginning reading. An understanding of the alphabetic principle is fundamental to skilled reading.

Every child enters the classroom with a unique set of literacy experiences. For some children, this means having had literally thousands of hours of book experience prior to entering the classroom. Others enter school with no book experience and with literacy experiences that are confined to observations of others interacting with print, such as paying the monthly bills, or interactions with the print in their environment, such as reading words on cereal boxes, traffic signs, or T-shirt logos. It is therefore hard to rationally accept a predetermined literacy curriculum. The task must be to evaluate what the child knows and begin to build an instructional program that meets the child's needs. Although a packaged literacy program may serve moderately well those children with an average amount of experience with books, it in no way meets the needs of children who are more or less able than their peers. In student-centered classrooms, instruction is based on the learning needs of children, not on the determinations of a set program.

This approach is contrasted with whole-class instruction based on a predetermined phonics curriculum. Whole-class phonics lessons seem to work best for those children who need them least. Conversely, children who most need to understand phonics seem to benefit least from whole-group lessons. Implementation of a whole-class approach to phonics instruction requires certain conditions to be in place for children to benefit from that instruction. Children need to understand that oral language is related to written language. This understanding develops with multiple experiences with a variety of texts.

In studies of children's emerging understandings about text, Ferreiro and Teberosky (1979) found that children went through a series of stages before developing the understanding that spoken language and written language are related. Initially, children understand a word in terms of its meaning. For example, *cat* is a four-legged furry animal that says meow. The word has no identity as a thing that can be examined outside of its meaning. At some point the child sees the word as a whole unit. Frith (1985) identified this as the *logographic stage.* As children's understanding develops, they begin to use individual letters and sounds to identify words. This is the *alphabetic stage.* In this stage, the word *cat* might initially be written as *k,* then *kt,* then *kat,* and finally *cat.* The last phase of development that Frith identifies is the *orthographic stage,* in which children see the patterns in words and explore words based on their origins rather than their sound-letter correspondences. As children reach this stage, the *at* in *cat* becomes a tool for reading and writing words such as *hat, that, baton,* or *matter.*

As children move toward understanding the sound structure of language, they begin to develop phonemic awareness. The development of phonemic awareness is not a linear process. Although there is a general continuum of difficulty among the phonemic awareness tasks that children can perform, the tasks can be learned concurrently rather than consecutively. For example, as children become phonemically aware, they do not need to learn to identify words that rhyme before they can learn to identify similar words that begin with the same sound, although the ability to recognize rhyme may precede the ability to identify similar sounds at the beginning of words. The same is true for the development of phonics. English-speaking children generally attend to initial consonant sounds first and are able to discriminate final consonant sounds later. Some children, however, attend to final consonant sounds first. Nor do children need to learn everything about phonemic awareness before they begin to learn about phonics.

The progress of any child is influenced by the quantity and quality of his or her interactions with adults around literacy, and that development is mediated by experiences with books. There is an interdependent relationship between the development of phonemic awareness and phonics knowledge and reading. Some phonemic awareness and phonics knowledge is helpful in beginning to read, and reading develops phonemic awareness and phonics knowledge (Perfetti, Beck, Bell, and Hughes, 1987).

For children who are having difficulty learning to read, it is important to build on what the student knows. In a predetermined curriculum or whole-group lessons, it is difficult to establish the links between known and unknown information that will support the struggling reader (Clay, 1993b).

The purpose of this book is to share the practices that have formed the core of phonics instruction in our classrooms. It is a snapshot of what goes on in our classrooms and an account of the techniques and strategies that have been successful in helping the children with whom we have worked. Our students represent the full range of learners a teacher might face in a primary classroom. There were children like Alicia, who was worried that perhaps she hadn't spelled *Caribbean* correctly in her first story written in first grade (she had), and Edward, who was unable to recognize his own name in print. Many of our students are labeled "special needs" children. As a group, they represent most, if not all, of the factors that put children at risk of reading failure. They reside in low-income families in poor neighborhoods, have limited proficiency in spoken English, have acquired less knowledge and skill pertaining to literacy during the preschool years, and lack age-appropriate skills in literacy-related abilities such as phonological awareness and general language ability (Snow, Burns, & Griffith, 1998). Despite these factors, our children have succeeded in learning to read. The structure and content of their instructional program, including phonics instruction, is instrumental in making this happen.

The Reading Process

The focus of this book is phonics. An understanding of phonics supports children as they learn to read. This understanding is one part of the reading process. Reading is a process of getting meaning from print. The skillful reader uses all of the tools available to him or her. These include all of the sources of information the reader can draw on: semantic information, syntactic information, and graphophonic information. *Semantic information* includes the form, context, and illustrations of the story. The background knowledge of the reader is a source of semantic information; the reader uses this information to check that reading makes sense. *Syntactic information* is the reader's understanding of the structure of language, how words combine to form sentences. The reader uses this information to check that reading sounds right, that reading sounds like talk. *Graphophonic information* is what the reader understands about letters and sounds and their relationship to each other. This includes an understanding of word patterns and word analogies. It is knowledge about the written alphabet and the sound structure of language. The reader uses this information to check that what is read looks right, that the sounds match the letters that are written. When all of the sources of information are used and the information from one source is checked against the others to ensure the text looks right, sounds right, and makes sense, the reader reaches the goal of meaningful reading.

If we teach children to use only one of these sources of information—whether it is the graphophonic, the syntactic, or the semantic—the child is unlikely to reach the goal of meaningful reading. To read efficiently, meaningfully, and fluently, children must be taught to use all of the information that is available to them as they read the text. One day when I was observing in a classroom, I sat down next to a first grader and asked if I could listen to him read some of his book. He nodded approval and set about the task. The text he was reading was Bill Martin Jr.'s (1967) *Brown Bear, Brown Bear, What Do You See?* With all the concentration he could muster he began *b, b, r, br, uh bruh, n, bruhn, brown, brown, b, b eh, beh, behr, bear.* At this point, the reading seemed to be almost painful, but I held back from intervening and allowed the child to continue assuming that he would now read the next phrase, a repetition of the first phrase, with fluency. I was totally surprised to find him beginning the same sounding-out behavior all over again. At this point I interrupted and asked if he could tell me this story. He responded with fluency and expression, "Oh, sure. Brown bear, brown bear, what do you see? I see a red bird looking at me." I told him that was wonderful and asked him, if that was what the story said, what he thought the words on this page might say. He seemed to be astounded by putting these two thoughts together and replied, "Oh, yeah. But when you read something, you have to sound it out." This story is not an indictment of phonics instruction. On the contrary, understanding letter-sound relationships and being able to apply them is essential to fluent reading. It is, however, an example of what can happen when only part of what the reader needs to understand is taught. When children read, they draw information from the illustrations in the text, the syntax of their spoken language, knowledge about story structure, context of the story, and their background knowledge, as well as from letter-sound information. Students need to be taught to use all of these sources of information or tools to get meaning from print.

Overreliance on any of the sources of information available to the reader to the exclusion of the others results in frustration for the reader or a lack of understanding of what is being read. Although students can continue to make progress for a limited amount of time, eventually lack of understanding will lead to lack of progress. As an example, one of my recent tasks was to assess the reading abilities of some first-grade students. Each child read leveled passages to me while I recorded their reading behaviors. Jason sat next to me and confidently began reading. When he came to the word *busy*, he began to sound it out. He blended the individual phonemes and arrived at *bus-ee*—not a word, but he seemed to have no expectation that it must be a word, or he assumed that somehow it was a word but he just didn't know it. He made similar errors when reading *shack* for *shake* and *sur-ee* for *sure*. The issue for this child was not a lack of understanding of letter-sound relationships; on the contrary, his errors demonstrate that he applied phonics rules exactly as he understood them. The larger problem was that the only source of information he was using was his understanding of phonics. What he didn't do was monitor his reading for meaning. If we can agree that the ultimate goal of all reading is to understand what is written, then it is imperative that we help children to see that phonics is a tool to help them unlock the meaning of the text rather than a set of letter-sound relationships and rules to be memorized and applied in isolation.

The question for us as teachers has always been how we can most effectively help children to learn phonics in a way that supports their reading development. In our classrooms, children are able to learn phonics and use that information in reading because the classroom environment, the instructional program, and the decisions of the teacher are focused on helping children to make meaningful connections between the skills of learning to read and the purposes for reading. Phonics is learned as a tool to be used in reaching the goal of meaningful reading.

Instructional Program

Our instructional program is built on a balanced foundation of teaching skills and teaching children to read for meaning. We begin to build that foundation by filling our classrooms with books: big books, little books, patterned books, rhyming books, easy books, difficult books, picture books, chapter books, fiction books, and nonfiction books. We read quality literature to our children. We read to them several times every day. We help them learn to love books so they will want to read on their own. As we're teaching them to love books, we teach them the skills and strategies they need to read the books they love. Neither skills nor reading for meaning is ever abandoned.

Concurrently, children are learning to write. They write every day on topics of their own choice. They create stories that tell about their lives, their interests, and the ideas that fill their imaginations. Children are developing their understanding of how letters and sounds work as they learn to encode their thoughts on paper. The phonics they learn as they are reading supports the work they do as writers. The phonics they learn as they are writing supports the problem solving they do as they are reading.

In order to make our classrooms as effective as possible, it is necessary to plan lessons that are multileveled and lessons that are differentiated. When activities are multileveled, they provide interest and challenge for the learner with emergent abilities as well as the learner whose abilities are more developed. Shared reading and shared writing are examples of multileveled activities. By planning a variety of instructional emphases, including the teaching of phonics relationships and generalizations, and by taking advantage of the teachable moments presented by the children, a teacher is able to meet the needs of a range of learners in a large-group lesson. Other lessons are differentiated based on ongoing assessment of student progress. Often it is not possible to meet the needs of the students in a large-group setting. In that case, information from ongoing assessment is used to group students for a focus lesson that specifically meets their learning needs. Focus lessons provide an opportunity for direct, explicit phonics instruction. The lesson is presented at a time when the members of the group will be able to learn the phonics relationship or generalization being taught and apply the information learned to the task of reading a new book or writing a story. Guided reading and interactive writing are examples of differentiated instruction.

Perhaps the most defining characteristic of our program for phonics instruction is that phonics is taught in the context of meaningful literacy experiences. Lessons begin and end with the text. This helps children to make a connection between the skills of reading and writing and the purposes of reading and writing. After a text has been read, a letter and sound being learned is introduced. Together, teacher and students examine the letter and related sound and draw conclusions about how and when to use this information. Students practice applying what they have learned with the support of the teacher and then return to the original text to apply this information to familiar material. Children may also be given similar material for independent practice. Skills are best learned through meaningful use. When children learn about phonics as they are reading or writing, they see the connections between letters, sounds, and texts. Instruction is focused on the use of phonics as a strategy for reading and writing. Strickland (1998) defines a strategy as a skill in use. We want our children not only to know the relationship between sounds and letters or the rules for using a long vowel sound or a short vowel sound in a word but also to apply this knowledge as they are reading and writing. We want our children to learn in a way that makes them better readers and writers each time they sit down with a book or a pencil and paper.

When children are taught phonics in context, they are able to draw on all of the sources of information available in the text, allowing them to confirm their prediction of a word being read. We could allow children to assume that the rules for applying sounds to letters were sufficient if there was enough consistency between the rules we have developed for sound-letter relationships. However, these relationships are notoriously unreliable. In a 1963 study, Clymer found that only 45% of the phonics rules that are commonly taught apply as often as 75% of the time. Teaching phonics in the context of reading allows students to use the rules or generalizations they have learned and check that the rule has held by arriving at a response that is meaningful and consistent with the structure of their spoken language.

Phonics instruction in our classrooms is direct and explicit. Children are taught the relationships between letters and sounds and use this information to read and write text. It is also systematic; however, the system is based on the abilities and needs of the students rather than on a predetermined curriculum. One of the things working with at-risk students has taught us is that there is no time to waste in the classroom. Reteaching letter-sound relationships that children already know and understand wastes precious time that should be spent on learning new information. In order to maximize the learning potential of each day, assessment becomes an integral component of instruction. Through observation, anecdotal records, and a variety of checklists, we chart our students' progress in learning and applying phonemic awareness and phonics knowledge to their reading and writing tasks.

The Teacher as a Key to Reading Success

Reading is a complex and multifaceted process, and children need an approach to reading that integrates many elements (Snow et al., 1998). Teaching reading is equally complex, and teachers need an in-depth knowledge of many techniques and strategies for effective instruction. It is important to recognize the critical role of a knowledgeable teacher in providing skilled reading instruction, including instruction in phonics. Knowledgeable teachers "effectively and deliberately plan their instruction to meet the diverse needs of children in a number of ways" (Snow et. al., 1998, p. 196). Planned, purposeful instruction that meets the needs of individual students is characteristic of phonics instruction in classrooms that take a balanced approach to literacy. The teacher makes instructional decisions about which phonics elements to teach based on what students need to learn to continue making progress in reading.

These instructional decisions are based not only on the teacher's assessments of student progress but also on the teacher's understanding of the development of language, the process of reading development, an understanding of text forms and functions, familiarity with instructional materials, and an understanding of models for instruction, including management of flexible grouping and differentiated instruction.

An understanding of the sound structure that underlies the English language and knowledge of the linguistic terms related to instruction may not be necessary in order to learn to read, but understanding language and how the elements work together in both spoken and written language will help teachers to make informed decisions when teaching children to read (Wilde, 1997). A significant part of what teachers must know is the vocabulary related to sounds and letters. Terms such as *phonology, orthography, phoneme, grapheme, schwa, digraph,* and *blend* are part of the vocabulary of language. Understanding these terms can facilitate a conversation about reading among the various groups interested in helping children to read better. With a common vocabulary and common definitions, our conversations can focus on the substance of reading instruction, and perhaps we will be able to find it easier to come to a consensus on reaching desired literacy outcomes. This will also allow teachers to engage in conversations with university researchers with the goal of making better use of research in the classroom, first by opening direct lines of communication and perhaps later by helping to define the research agenda so that the research has more immediate and meaningful outcomes for the classroom. This will also make it possible for teachers to explain their thinking about reading instruction and phonics to parents, administrators, and community groups.

Researchers have tried to determine the best method for teaching reading. Studies have also begun to try to determine the best materials for reading instruction. Rather than looking for the single best method or materials, time might better be spent in evaluating methods and materials on a variety of criteria to help teachers match materials to the needs of each child. This type of evaluation would allow teachers to make the best possible teaching decisions for each child. The answer to how to best teach children to read is not in a single book or even in a single series of books. The answer lies in experienced teachers who know that different children have different learning needs. To ensure that all children are successful, the teaching decisions about what to teach, in what order, and when to teach it must be left to skilled classroom teachers. Teaching young children to read must be taken seriously. Skilled teachers using a variety of good materials and applying their best professional judgment about the interaction of timely instruction with those materials is the best plan for helping children to learn to read. Especially for those children who find it more difficult to learn to read, this requires a teacher with knowledge and experience.

Limiting teachers to whole-class instruction and a single set of materials guarantees uniform instruction, but is uniform instruction the way to optimal learning? One of the things we can be completely sure of is that children are not uniform. They are unique and they require a teacher who will respond instructionally to that uniqueness. Does that mean that there are no general principles that can be taught or that should be learned? Of course not, but the best way to guarantee success for the most children is to have a teacher who knows reading and knows the children and combines this information to maximize their learning potential. It is the depth of the teacher's knowledge and his or her ability to apply that knowledge to the unique challenges of the individual students that will make the significant difference in reading achievement for children.

In one of my former classes, there were two wonderful little girls. In many ways, Amy and Amanda were as alike as two little girls can be. They had dark hair, bright eyes, and shy but infectious giggles. They entered first grade ready to take on the challenge of reading. As Amanda told me, "I know my letters and I can read a little," to which Amy added, "Me too." Both girls came from warm, caring families. Their moms and dads had been reading to them since they were very small, and they loved being read to. The families made regular visits to the library, and books were part of their homes. They took family trips to places like the zoo, botanical gardens, and natural history museum.

Amy and Amanda had attended the same preschool, and both had many of the early literacy experiences that we know are important to the foundation children need to become readers. They even had the same kindergarten teacher. When they entered first grade, they knew all the letters of the alphabet and had an emerging sense of sound-letter relationships. They were able to read a few simple books that were at the same level of difficulty. With so many similar experiences and such similar competencies, in most classrooms the girls would have been put in the same group for reading. Although it is true the girls had similar competencies, they approached text very differently.

Amanda understood the relationships between sounds and letters. When coming to an unknown word, she invariably chose to sound the word out. In fact, initially she tried to sound out every word she came to, including words she had previously read in the same story. As a result, the pace of her reading was slow and she would lose track of the meaning of the story. She could use what she understood about phonics, but by itself this was an ineffective strategy for reading.

Amy knew that reading should make sense and it should sound like a story. She used pictures as clues and relied on her sense of story structure to construct a story to fit the pictures. Although Amy knew all the letters of the alphabet and most of the sound associations for the letters, she made only minimal attempts to match the sounds to the letters in the words of the text. She was using all of the semantic information in the text, but because it was all she was using, her reading was also ineffective.

These two girls were similar in the level of books they were reading but very different in their processing of the text. The instructional decisions for these children had to consider more than their reading level; it was also necessary to reflect on their strategy use. For both girls to learn to read and read well, they needed an instructional program that supported their strengths while explicitly teaching them the skills and strategies they were not yet using. Reading is more than sounding out words. Reading is more than looking at pictures. A knowledgeable teacher will draw on a wide range of instructional techniques to help every child learn to read successfully.

CHAPTER 2

What Does Phonics Instruction Look Like in the Classroom?

Jonathan enters the kindergarten classroom and puts his jacket and backpack away. He returns to the sign-in center and takes his name card from the name chart. He chooses a pencil and carefully writes his name in the class log on the page for today's date. Amy has already signed in and is sitting in the reading corner with her friend Maris. The girls are reading *Is Your Mama A Llama?* (Guarino, 1991), a story the teacher read aloud to the class yesterday. Juan Carlos sits in the rocking chair. His eyes search the pages of *Dinosaurs, Dinosaurs* (Barton, 1989). Andre and Daniel read today's menu, marking their lunch choice on the order form. They check to see how many children are having chicken nuggets and how many are having peanut butter. As the rest of the children finish signing in and making choices for the day, Mrs. Francis talks with the children. She inquires about their health, their families, and their interests. This is her opportunity to settle the children into the routine for the day and bridge the space between school and home.

On a signal from Mrs. Francis, the children assemble on the rug. Mrs. Francis begins by asking the children which of a selection of favorite books they would like to read today. They choose *I Went Walking* by Sue Williams (1990). The children have read this story many times, so they read the book with enthusiasm and confidence. After the reading, Mrs. Francis gives a few children the opportunity to come to the book and identify the letter *w* in the text. She and the children say the *w* words together and listen to the sound they hear at the beginning of those words. When the children have finished, Mrs. Francis places the big book *Who Will Be My Mother?* (Cowley, 1990) on the book stand. This is a new book, so Mrs. Francis and the children discuss what they think the book might be about and look at the pictures to get a sense of the story before they begin reading. Mrs.

Francis invites the children to listen to the story as she reads. She wants the children to hear the story read with fluency, phrasing, and expression. The children discuss the story, expressing their opinions about what part of the book they liked and why. During the discussion, Mrs. Francis encourages the children to recount the events in the story. When the children have finished discussing the story, Mrs. Francis explains the center activities for the day.

Mrs. Francis has planned center activities to encourage the children to develop their language and literacy skills. She and the children have worked hard over the past several weeks to develop the routines and expectations for center activities. The children were given many opportunities to practice and discuss appropriate behaviors for centers. Emily and Evan go to the flannel board, where they use flannel cutouts of the story characters to retell *Who Will Be My Mother?* Delia, Fran, and Margaret are reading individual copies of *Who Will Be My Mother?* They reread the story in unison, supporting each other as they read. Margaret has transitioned from emergent to conventional reading, and she takes the lead when the group comes to an unfamiliar word. Franklin, Juan Carlos, and Andre choose to work at the alphabet center. Andre matches foam letter cutouts with the letters on an alphabet strip. Juan Carlos and Franklin test each other by holding up plastic letters for the other to identify. In the block center, Mrs. Francis has placed a copy of *Who Will Be My Mother?* and a little stuffed lamb, the main character in the story. Travis, Michael, and Daniel build a barn for the little lamb, checking the picture to be sure they are making the right shape. Mrs. Francis glances around the room, assures herself that all of the children are productively engaged, and makes a few anecdotal notes on the activities the children have chosen. Children are reading big books, sorting pictures by initial sound at the pocket chart, writing letters in the post office, and listening to stories on tape. Mrs. Francis calls Robert, Elena, Stephanie, and Martin to the front of the room, where they play a rhyming game together. After the rhyming game, Mrs. Francis asks another group of children to join her. This group reads a poem together, then uses Wikki Stix™ to identify specific letters. As the children identify the letters, Mrs. Francis makes notes in her notebook to chart progress with letter identification. These children return to their centers, and a new group joins Mrs. Francis. This group has a guided reading lesson on an emergent level book entitled *Kitty and the Birds* (Randell, 1994). The children finish their lesson and go off to read the book in pairs. Mrs. Francis checks the time and notes that it's almost time for the children to begin their snack. She makes a few final notes about the group in her notebook and signals cleanup time.

When planning for phonics and phonemic awareness instruction based on the needs of children, a teacher must consider what that instruction looks like. An effective teacher plans the classroom environment. He or she considers the physical arrangement of the class, the materials needed for learning, and the necessary routines to give the students a variety of learning opportunities. Students have opportunities to participate in whole-class, small-group, and individual instruction. The teacher plans a classroom environment that promotes and supports teaching and learning.

The Classroom Environment

A classroom environment that supports children in learning about phonics and using that information in texts is rich in opportunities for learning about print. This means that everything from the alphabet strips on students' desks to print displayed on the walls for students to read is done in a way that supports their learning. Things as simple as using the same key word with the alphabet displayed on the wall and the alphabet strip on the students' desks can make the connection between sound and letter easier for some children to learn. Placing print such as alphabet charts at the children's eye level promotes easy use. The print environment is not only rich but also purposeful. Print materials are placed in the environment when the teacher has evaluated the students' need for the materials and their ability to use the materials effectively. Print in the classroom environment changes with the development and needs of the children. Displays become more complex as children add to them throughout the year. These print materials include interactive word walls where students add words to alphabetized charts. These words may be the children's names, high-frequency words for reading and writing, or words from a content unit of study. Print materials may also include poems on charts, labels in the classroom library, and posted messages written by the teacher and the students. Students are taught to use the print in the environment, which provides a reference for the children as they practice literacy skills that have been recently learned. Environmental print also gently nudges children toward learning new skills and strategies. Figures 2-1 and 2-2 illustrate print-rich classes.

Figure 2-1. Collections of books in the print-rich environment

Figure 2-2. Word charts in the print-rich environment

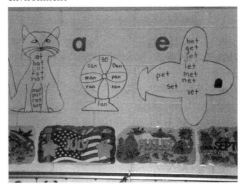

The classroom environment includes opportunities for demonstrations of how print works and opportunities to practice applying what is being learned with support or independently. In discussing the importance of a balanced reading program, Margaret Mooney (1990) suggests opportunities for reading to children, reading with children, and reading by children as part of the daily classroom routine. This includes the opportunity to listen to stories being read aloud. Reading aloud to children helps them to understand story structure, develops background knowledge, and increases vocabulary. Children develop a sense of the sounds of language and phonological awareness as they listen to stories being read. Reading with children, as in shared reading, provides demonstrations of skilled reading and an opportunity to practice applying reading skills with the support of the teacher. Children develop sight vocabulary, form generalizations about word patterns, and apply their understanding of phonics relationships to the stories they are reading. Reading by children gives them the opportunity to orchestrate the strategies they are learning, cross-checking one source of information with another. Repeated reading of texts builds sight vocabulary and automaticity with words and word parts. Independent reading of texts with the appropriate level of challenge develops fluency. Reading to, reading with, and reading by children helps them to understand the relationship between letters and sounds, develops background knowledge, increases vocabulary, develops strategies for monitoring comprehension, and develops fluency. Cumulatively, these are the key factors in continued reading development (Snow et. al., 1998). Figures 2-3 and 2-4 illustrate reading by children.

The classroom environment is rich in opportunities to develop oral language. The strength of a child's oral language ability is the strength of his or her foundation for reading. The quantity and quality of the conversation in a class-

Figure 2-3. Children need time for independent reading every day

Figure 2-4. Comfortable spaces encourage reading by children

room contributes to the reading achievement of the students. A rich oral language environment contributes to the development of phonemic awareness as songs, rhymes, and chants are heard. It contributes to the development of vocabulary as stories and informational text are read and discussed. It contributes to phonics knowledge as students work on reading messages together and writing shared stories. Children use their knowledge of oral language to check both the correctness of decoding and the comprehension of text. They ask if this is a real word and if it makes sense in this passage as they are reading.

The classroom environment is rich in opportunities to write. Writing allows children to experience the communicative purpose of print as they construct messages. Children's writing shows the teacher what children understand about sounds, letters, and words. The teacher demonstrates writing in front of the children to provide them with a model for composing, spelling, and applying knowledge of sounds and letters to writing. Children also have the opportunity for writing in a writing center (Figure 2-5). In shared writing, children work with the teacher to apply their knowledge of sounds, letters, and words to compose a message (Figure 2-6). Modeling and shared writing prepare the children for independent writing. Children write independently each day on topics of their own choice.

Classroom environments that promote learning allow students to feel safe

Figure 2-5. The writing center invites children to use phonics knowledge for authentic purposes

Figure 2-6. Shared writing helps children transition to independent writing

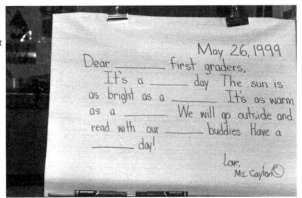

and supported. Students' attempts to learn are respected. This means that the teacher values what the students do and uses information about their attempts to help them learn even more. After attending a recent professional conference, a colleague shared this story about a child who was trying to determine which of a variety of objects began with the letter *w.* As the child worked on her task, she continually considered, then discarded, the picture of the window in favor of others. Sensing that this was in some way bothering the child, an observer in the class asked the child to tell her about what she was doing. The child explained the task correctly and then with some concern related that the teacher had said that *window* starts with a *w,* but it couldn't be *window* because *window* starts with an *l.* The observer continued to listen to the child as she began to make a vertical line and a horizontal line. "See," she replied, "It starts with an *l.*" Vignettes such as this demonstrate how easily a child's learning can be blocked by confusion. In classrooms where children learn best about phonics, or any other skill or content, children are given opportunities to make attempts that are valued and to explain their thinking about those attempts to allow the teacher to make better instructional decisions. In this case, the teacher was able to reevaluate the task and see that the child was unable to differentiate between the real object and the phonemes of the word used to represent the object. This information can be used to support the child's learning by developing more appropriate literacy tasks.

Another key component of classroom environment is gauging the amount of support that students are given as they take on new challenges. Guided by the work of Vygotsky (1962), the teacher structures learning experiences so that what a child is asked to do today with support, he or she is able to do tomorrow independently. This requires the teacher to be aware of the daily emerging abilities and changing capabilities of their children. A variety of ongoing assessments makes this possible. Students are supported as they take on new challenges, and the level of that support is changed as the student becomes more able to do the task independently. Marie Clay (1991) advises to never do for learners what they can do for themselves. Structuring instruction so that children are working at the edge of their ability keeps frustration low and motivation high. Motivation is a significant factor in helping children to become skilled readers (Snow et al., 1998).

Classroom Materials

The Classroom Library

The classroom environment is rich in the number and variety of books in the classroom library. The books cover a wide range of subjects by a variety of authors and illustrators across a range of reading levels. It contains class-made books, individual student-made books, teacher-made books, and trade books. The books represent many genres, including realistic fiction, fairy tales, fables, fantasy, alphabet books, counting books, concept books, biography, mystery, nonfiction, poetry, dictionaries and other reference books.

The library contains books that are easy to read. Books such as *Cat on the Mat* (Wildsmith, 1982), and *Spring Snow* (Smith, 1998) give children strong support as they are beginning their journey as independent readers. Such books have strong picture support, patterned text, and easily decodable words.

The library also contains books with increasing levels of challenge such as *The Bear's Bicycle* (McLeod, 1975) and *A Friend for Dragon* (Pilkey, 1994). These books have an expanded story line and less picture support and require children to apply their increasing knowledge of phonics and structural analysis to their reading. The books provide opportunities for students to learn about phonics and structural analysis and to apply what they are learning as they read. Finally, the library contains books that are challenging for the young reader. Books such as *The Relative's Came* (Rylant, 1985) and *Horrible Harry and the Dungeon* (Kline, 1998) support the reader with familiar subject matter but require the application of a range of skills and strategies to read the text accurately. The books provide opportunities for students to apply what they know about how print works and to orchestrate the use of strategies to become fluent readers.

The books are displayed in ways that allow children to make good choices for the purposes of their reading, whether they are practicing reading to develop fluency or obtaining information about a topic of interest. The teacher may label books in the classroom library according to topic, author, or genre. Storing books for easy use is important. The teacher can use labeled baskets, bins, or other attractive containers to hold the books, which can then be easily returned to the place where they belong. The teacher includes books at varying levels of difficulty in each of these baskets. In this way, students at different reading levels can practice reading skills with material of high interest to them.

In addition to books, the classroom library includes other reading materials such as newspapers and magazines. *Babybug, Ladybug, The Mini Page, Ranger Rick, Highlights for Children,* and *Zoo World* are examples of newspapers and magazines that appeal to young learners.

Figures 2-7 and 2-8 show well-organized classroom libraries.

Figure 2-7. Library organization makes choosing a book easy

Figure 2-8. Classroom libraries are well-organized and labeled clearly

Other Print Materials

In preschool and early primary classrooms, big books are essential print material. Big books are ideal for shared reading experiences for the whole class or for small groups of children. Using a big book allows children to see the text as the teacher points to the words when she reads aloud. This helps beginning readers to understand how print works and that sounds and letters make words that in turn make sentences and stories. Big books provide a print model the teacher uses for instruction of phonics and structural analysis. Sounds, letters, and words are studied within the context of meaningful print.

In addition to big books, classrooms contain the same titles in little book format. The little books give children the opportunity to independently read the story they listened to the teacher read. The classroom also contains many sets of little books that are used for guided reading lessons. These little books are leveled. The level indicates the amount of challenge the text presents to the young reader. Each child in a guided reading group will have an individual copy of the text to use during instruction.

Listening centers are created with books and matching audiotapes. In such centers children have the opportunity to see the words as they listen to a story being read. Listening to books on tape provides children with a model of skilled reading. The opportunity to examine the print as the story is read allows children to make connections to lessons on letters and sounds as well as to make discoveries about the letters and sounds of the text on their own.

Reading games provide opportunities for students to practice applying what they have learned about sounds, letters, words, and strategies. Games such as Alphabet Bingo, Boggle Junior™, Junior Scrabble™, I Spy, and Green Eggs and Ham create opportunities for children to manipulate the elements that build fluent reading in playful settings. Teacher-made games such as Letter Bingo, Concentration, and Go Fish should also be available.

Manipulatives

The classroom environment offers children a variety of ways to learn about letters and sounds, including working with materials that can be manipulated (Figure 2-9). Children learning about letters and sounds are young and approach the world very concretely. To learn about letters, they will need experiences that are concrete in nature, experiences with materials that have substance, texture, and dimension. Many classrooms contain sets of letters made from a variety of materials: felt, plastic, foam, wood, and sandpaper. Magnetic letters and letter tiles are another way for children to work with letters in a concrete way. All of these letter sets can be used for tracing, matching, and sorting. They can be moved together and taken apart in order to demonstrate how letters are sequenced to form words, how by changing a word onset, the part of the word before the vowel, you can make word patterns, and how by changing the affix of a word you can make word families.

Figure 2-9. Children work with alphabet manipulatives

Writing Materials

Writing letters and words is less concrete than working with textured and three-dimensional letters, but it is no less important. As children are learning about print, it is essential that they have opportunities to make letters and words using a variety of media. The classroom has a supply of brushes and paint, pens, markers, crayons, colored pencils, chalk, small chalkboards, sand trays, and dry erase markers and boards. Children use the materials to make letters and words. The variety of these experiences helps to imprint the letters in the students' minds and builds automatic and fluent recognition of the letter.

Other materials that invite children to write are stationery, envelopes, postcards, sticky notes, and paper in a variety of sizes, textures, and colors. The classroom contains premade blank books to encourage and inspire the students to write. Some of these books are as simple as folded paper, others are stapled or spiral-bound and covered with contact paper or decorative paper. Children enjoy writing in shape books and flip books. A computer and printer equipped with software for word processing and creating graphics promote student writing. The teacher helps the children to match the kind of book with what most suits their writing. By writing stories, informational pieces, poems, biographies, or other text, children practice what they know about sounds, letters, conventions of print, and text organization. Writing reinforces what they learn about reading.

Figure 2-10 illustrates this type of writing center.

Figure 2-10. Children using an alphabet chart for their writing

Routines

Establishing routines is a critical part of the classroom environment that supports learning. Children need predictable routines to function responsibly and productively in the classroom. The teacher needs to establish routines so that there is time to meet with children in small groups and individually during the day. Expectations for classroom behavior, procedures, and academic tasks must be modeled and clearly explained. When the teacher is meeting with a small group of children, the rest of the children in the class know what to do so that the small-group instruction is not interrupted. The same is true for one-on-one instruction.

The teacher plans and explains procedures for basic classroom routines such as the following:

- Beginning the school day
- Retrieving, using, and returning materials, such as books, pencils, different kinds of paper, and art materials
- Using equipment, such as the pencil sharpener and overhead projector
- Working in centers or designated areas of the room
- Employing independent work habits such as obtaining supplies, completing assignments, moving around the room, and following procedures when the teacher is instructing a small group or an individual student
- Attending to the teacher's signals, such as a bell, timer, hand clap, or music on tape
- Following the procedures for taking care of personal needs, such as physical needs, questions, and conflicts with other students

- Completing class jobs

When procedures and routines are clearly established and practiced, the children are free to concentrate on learning. The teacher can concentrate on instruction based on the strengths and needs of the students rather than losing valuable instructional time to solve procedural and behavioral issues. Figure 2-11 shows a sample chart.

Figure 2-11. Good readers chart

Schedules

The teacher plans a predictable schedule (Figure 2-12) that provides a framework for instruction. Although the teacher often cannot dictate the time when lunch, physical education, music, and other special classes are held, he or she can plan how to use the time in the classroom. When planning a schedule, the teacher needs to consider the times of whole-class, small-group, and individual instruction as well as the children's need to move and, therefore, plans for activities that allow the children to move about after sitting for a time. Schedules should provide many opportunities for children to read, write, speak, and listen. The teacher plans a schedule that creates flexibility within blocks of time and that allows for making connections and weaving concepts together throughout the day. Young learners need repetition in ways that allow them to see connections and patterns. For example, when learning phonics, a child is introduced to the sounds and letters at the beginning of words. In one day, the teacher may present this during shared reading and reinforce it throughout the day—during an individual reading lesson, a group guided reading lesson, and a writing lesson. The teacher also reinforces the concepts during dismissal by having the children line up according to the first letter of their names.

Figure 2-12. The daily schedule is posted for children's reference

Figure 2-13, a schedule for a block of time dedicated to language arts instruction, shows how the time might be divided and what might be included depending on the needs of the students.

Figure 2-13. Sample Language Arts Schedule—Preschool and Kindergarten

8:30–8:50	Children arrive at school and prepare for the day; unpack backpack, sign in, and choose a center.
8:50–9:20	Reading instruction • Shared reading—including instruction on letter identification, phonemic awareness, and phonics • Focus lesson
9:20–9:50	Center activities • Buddy reading • Reading response • Independent reading • Retelling activities • Alphabet activities • Phonemic awareness and phonics games (During center time the teacher may interact with the children in the centers to support and extend their learning or may work with small groups and individual children on language arts tasks where assessment has demonstrated the need for instruction.) Guided reading (small-group and individual) Phonemic awareness activities Assessment
9:50–10:00	Snack and read-aloud
10:00–10:40	Writing instruction • Shared writing such as morning message, class news, including instruction on letter identification, phonemic awareness, and phonics • Focus lesson • Independent writing 　—Journal 　—Log 　—Story 　—Poem 　—Informational piece (During independent writing the teacher works with children individually or in small groups to reinforce or extend their understanding of letter-sound relationships or the writing process. This may include interactive writing lessons with individual children.) Interactive writing Writing conferences Assessment
10:40–11:00	Sharing Assessment

Figure 2-14 shows a similar schedule for higher grades.

Figure 2-14. Sample Language Arts Schedule—Kindergarten–Third Grade

8:30–8:50	Children arrive at school and prepare for the day; unpack backpack, sharpen pencils, and get materials. Some teachers ask children to complete a warm-up activity or read independently until opening procedures are completed.
8:50–9:50	Reading instruction • Shared reading • Focus lesson—including instruction on letter identification, phonics, and word analysis (Following whole-group activities, the teacher works with small groups and individual students in guided reading groups or reading conferences.) • Guided reading (small-group and individual) • Reading conferences • Independent reading • Buddy reading • Reading response • Assessment (part of each component of reading instruction)
9:50–10:00	Break
10:00–11:00	Writing instruction • Shared writing such as morning message, class news, including instruction on letter identification, phonics, and word analysis • Focus lesson (During independent writing the teacher works with children individually or in small groups to reinforce or extend their understanding of letter-sound relationships or the writing process. This may include interactive writing lessons with individual children.) • Independent writing —Journal —Log —Story —Poem —Informational piece • Research • Conferences for revision and editing • Interactive writing • Assessment (part of each component of writing instruction)

These samples show the many components of effective reading and writing instruction. The teacher allots time as needed for the purposes of the lesson and orchestrates a variety of activities that promote literacy learning, including phonics. It is important that schedules and routines be as predictable as possible so that children can anticipate and respond with appropriate learning behaviors.

The students enter Mrs. Norton's third-grade classroom. They hang up their coats and backpacks, retrieving pencils, papers, and books from the packs. They turn in their homework to a basket marked "Homework." As the children settle into their seats, they take journals out of their desks and begin to write about the books they are reading. After taking attendance and lunch count, Mrs. Norton begins reading *The Egyptian Cinderella* (Climo, 1989), a short story related to the social studies unit of Ancient Egypt. After she finishes reading, she and the children discuss the story. Mrs. Norton places a copy of one of the pages on the overhead projector. Mrs. Norton has noted that her students are inconsistent in the correct use of past tense in their writing. She wants to review and reinforce this skill. Together, she and the students find verbs indicating past tense. She highlights the words, discussing their meanings with the children. They discuss why some words have *-ed* endings and some do not. She then assigns the students to find past tense verbs in their independent reading. Mrs. Norton reviews the tasks for the reading part of language arts time. She plans to meet with two small groups and listen to several children read individually. When they are not meeting with her, the students are to continue reading their independent reading books, find past tense verbs and vocabulary words related to the study of Egypt, complete their journal entries, and work on drafts of their information pieces about ancient Chinese contributions. As they identify verbs and vocabulary words, the students write the words on sticky note paper and stick them on charts around the room.

Mrs. Norton meets with a group of five students for a guided reading lesson. She has chosen this group because they need to work on applying their knowledge of word parts to determine unknown words. They are reading a book about ancient Egyptians. She says the word *preserved* and asks the children to find it on a page. She notes that all but one child finds the word. Jose helps Henry to find it.

"What parts or syllables do you see in this word?"

"I see an *-ed* ending," says Marie.

"Good, what else do you see?"

"I see the word *serve*," answers Jose.

"Good, put your fingers around that little word. How can you use that word to help you when you read *preserved*?"

"I can say *serve* and connect it to the rest of the word when I say the letters," replies Jenny.

"If I can say *serve*, I can say the rest of the word," states Jose.

"We know the prefix *pre-*, too," says Jenny.

"Yes, you do, so we can figure this word out by looking at the parts," Mrs. Norton explains.

The children and Mrs. Norton discuss how the Egyptians preserved mummies. They go on to find other words and discuss them. Mrs. Norton dismisses this group to read the selection independently or with a buddy. She circulates around the room checking on the students' progress with their tasks. Children are contributing the words *pyramids*, *pharaohs*, and *irrigation* to the word charts. They are adding the verbs *found, hurried,* and *twirled.* One child places *shout* on the verb list. Mrs. Norton makes a note for future discussion. She calls Zach up to her table. He brings two books with him. He is reading a book that he says is easy, and he has another one that he thinks is just right. Previously, Mrs. Norton taught her students how to choose books that they would be able to read. While she listens to Zach read from the easy book, she takes notes. Zach is correct; it is easy. She asks him to read from the more challenging book. Zach reads with less confidence, misreading some words. Mrs. Norton notes those words and asks Zach to go back to them. He misread the words *position* and *lunkhead.* Mrs. Norton talks to Zach about the ending *-tion* and how he can use it to figure out the first word. She shows him that *lunkhead* is a compound word. They discuss the meaning. Mrs. Norton sends Zach off and asks him to continue reading *The Kid in the Red Jacket* (Park, 1987) for next time.

Mrs. Norton meets with another child individually, also taking notes and providing instruction. She then meets with the second group. After that, she meets individually with two more children. She ends the reading time with a whole-class discussion of the words the children chose for the charts and why they chose them. She collects journals from six children. She will read and respond in writing to them later.

Mrs. Norton plans with the children for writing conferences and independent writing. This block of time follows reading. During this time, she meets with individual children and small groups. She meets with one group of children to discuss content revisions to their information writing, then she meets with a group of children whose writing demonstrated inconsistency of verb tense. She asks them to read over their pieces and check where they need *-ed* endings. She reminds them that finding words that need endings is like finding the past tense words in their independent reading. Mrs. Norton observes the children as they correct their writing.

She notes the children who are having difficulty and plans to meet with them individually. After meeting with the groups, Mrs. Norton circulates around the room, stopping to meet with children for individual conferences. Whenever possible, Mrs. Norton makes connections between what the children know about reading to their writing. She asks Aimee to think about how authors of books show action. She reminds Omar that he can look at a book to see how authors use verb tense. Milad asks her to spell a word, and she asks him to think about the sounds he hears when he says the word slowly.

"C-o-n-t-r-b-u, oh, I know *shun,* it's like the end of *nation.*" He quickly writes *t-i-o-n.*

"Good connection to what you know. That's what good readers and writers do, and you almost have it," Mrs. Norton comments. She then asks Milad to count out the syllables. He taps them and realizes that there is a letter missing after the *r.* With Mrs. Norton's help he determines that it should be an *i.*

Mrs. Norton closes the writing block with a few of the students reading part of their pieces aloud to the class. The students and Mrs. Norton note how the student authors use techniques like those of the authors of the books they read. Jose remarks how much he likes Kate's action words, and Mrs. Norton points out how well Marie fixed the verb tense in her writing.

CHAPTER 3

Phonological Awareness

Children's ability to read is built upon a strong foundation of oral language. This foundation has many building blocks. Children learn the structure of language as they use it to communicate their wants and needs to others. They develop vocabulary as they talk to adults and other children, listen to stories being read, and comment on the world around them. They develop the understanding that language is composed of sounds, words, and phrases as they discover language in poems, recite rhymes, and sing songs.

Children explore language in the same way that they explore the rest of their world. They watch, they listen, they develop a theory on how things work, and they try things out. Observe young children building towers of blocks. They stack them up only to watch them tumble down and then rebuild the tower all over again, this time in a more stable configuration. With every building, children refine their theories on how to balance the blocks and develop new understandings of how to build a stable tower. This same process is very much at work as children develop phonological awareness. They sort out speech sounds from other sounds in the environment. They begin to understand the relationship between speech sounds and the results of that speech. With time and experience, most children begin to understand that language can be explored and manipulated as an object itself rather than as part of a message. Children note that their name starts like a relative's name. They sing nonsense rhymes to themselves as they engage in other activities, rhymes like *Ben, hen, fen* or *Jason, mason, tason*. They comment that *centipede* is a big word and *bird* is a small word. They notice these things long before they are familiar with written language and can visually see the differences or similarities in the words. This ability to examine language as an object of thought, to explicitly examine language in terms of its form and structure rather than its meaning, is *phonological awareness.* When children notice that words rhyme, begin and end with the same sound, or have varying lengths, they are developing phonological awareness. *Phonemic awareness,* the ability to consciously reflect on and manipulate the individual sounds or phonemes of a word, is part of phonological awareness and develops later as children explore language in greater and greater detail.

There are many paths to reading, but somewhere between children's first encounters with books and the time when they become skilled readers, children must learn to effectively use the alphabetic principle. They must learn that the sounds of English are paired with letters and that those sounds are the same sounds that we use when we speak. This understanding is neither obvious nor, in some cases, easy to learn. When children do not develop phonological awareness, they are at risk of reading failure (Adams, 1990). Children who perform well on phonological awareness tasks in kindergarten and first grade are more likely to become successful readers (Bradley & Bryant, 1983, 1985; Catts, 1991; Mann, 1994).

Most children develop phonological awareness as they listen to stories being read, learn to recite nursery rhymes, sing songs, and engage in language play. Approximately 75% of middle-class first graders develop phonological awareness without direct instruction (Adams, 1990). This number is considerably smaller for other demographic groups. Because phonological awareness is such a strong predictor of reading achievement (Blachman, 1991; Juel, 1991; Stanovich, 1986; Wagner, Torgesen, & Raschotte, 1994), a strong emphasis is being placed on developing phonological awareness in the preschool years. Phonological awareness can be developed in preschool settings for those children who have not learned it on their own. Preschool programs should immerse children in purposeful, language-rich environments. In very similar ways to those children who develop phonological awareness independently, the preschool program of games, songs, stories, and poems that emphasize the sounds and structure of language should be woven into the fabric of daily instruction. The teacher makes the phonological aspects of these activities explicit to the children.

Phonological awareness activities move children from exploring language for its meaning to developing knowledge of its form and structure. Children need many opportunities to use language and to think about the language they are using before this knowledge develops. They begin to understand that some sounds are the same and some are different, that sounds can be compared, and that the order of sounds is important. There is no set age at which children begin to develop phonological awareness, and the level of phonological awareness varies from child to child (Bradley & Bryant, 1985; Maclean, Bryant, & Bradley, 1987). One of the first aspects of phonological awareness that children learn is rhyme. Goswami and Bryant (1990) found that children are sensitive to rhyme at a very early age. In exploring the relationship between knowledge of nursery rhymes and the phonological skills needed for early reading, children as young as 3 were found to have a knowledge of rhymes (Maclean et al., 1987). By the end of kindergarten most children can produce rhyming words.

As children are becoming phonologically aware, they begin to attend to smaller units of sound. Very young children develop an awareness of syllables without formal instruction (Winner, Landerl, Linortner, & Hummer, 1991). Gradually, young children begin to attend to the initial phoneme and the spoken syllable (Adams, 1990; Moustafa, 1997; Treiman, 1986; Treiman and Baron, 1981; Treiman and Chafetz, 1987). After a year of kindergarten most children are able to identify and segment words into syllables and delete the first syllable of a multi syllabic word (Liberman, Shankweiler, Fischer, & Carter, 1974; Stanovich, Cunningham, & Cramer, 1984; Yopp, 1988).

Phonological Awareness Throughout the Day

Researchers have demonstrated that phonological awareness can be taught. This is important because a large number of children who enter classrooms today have not had the opportunity to develop phonological awareness. The ability to attend to and examine the sounds of our language is not a skill that must be learned within a limited window of opportunity or the opportunity is lost. From the very first day of school, teachers begin helping children to develop this important strategy for becoming a successful reader. The ideal materials for helping children to develop phonological awareness are the books, poems, songs, and games that are the core of a good preschool or kindergarten curriculum. Group time that includes shared reading of books such as Bruce Degen's (1990) *Jamberry,* recitation of nursery rhymes, singing "Eency Weency Spider," and playing games where children match pictures of objects whose names rhyme are excellent for developing phonological awareness.

Children learn best when they are learning in meaningful contexts. This is as true for developing a sense of phonological awareness as for any other part of the curriculum. Therefore, to the extent possible, the activities used for teaching phonological awareness should be an integrated part of the instructional program. If the teaching goal is to focus on listening to help children attend to sounds, then this should be done in a way that fits with the rest of what is being learned. For example, when children are studying the farm, listening games in which children are asked to identify the sounds of farm animals would be appropriate. Teachers might read books that focus on the sounds farm animals make, such as *The Farm Concert* by Joy Cowley (1990a). Especially for those children who have the most difficulty learning, it is important to make explicit the connections between what they know and what they are trying to learn.

Listening

As a first step in helping children to develop a sense of the sounds of our language, it is useful to help them develop listening skills. Listening is easily taken for granted. We are surrounded by sound and often assume that listening is something everyone can do. However, listening with attention is a skill that individuals develop. The very active listening that children will need when applying what they know about letter-sound relationships in reading and writing is quite different from the listening that children do when watching a favorite television program. In reading and writing, we want children to be active listeners, to listen with attention and analyze the sounds they are hearing.

There are many similarities between learning to speak and learning to read. One of these similarities is the importance of listening to learning. When children are learning to speak, they are active listeners. They are attentive to the language sounds and patterns of those around them, as well as to the vocabulary and the intended meaning of the speech of those individuals. They analyze what is being said and how it is being said in order to become participants in the conversation and to make their needs known. As children become facile with speech, they become less attentive to the sounds and patterns of language and more focused on the meaning of what is being said. As children transition from oral to written language, we want them to move from examining language for its meaning to examining language for its underlying sound structure. This means that children once again need to listen to language "actively, attentively, and analytically" (Adams, Foorman, Lundberg, & Beeler, 1998).

If we want children to become active listeners, we must first create contexts in which listening is important and then demonstrate for children what we mean by listening. Listening, like any other skill we want children to learn, should be modeled. One of the most purposeful contexts for teaching listening in early childhood is during circle, when children are sharing the processes and products of their work for the day. During this time, children are focused on listening to each other as they explain their efforts. To help children use this time effectively, teachers demonstrate what good listening looks like and sounds like. Teachers prompt children with statements that focus student attention on listening to the speaker. "I really want to hear how Carla made this painting. I wonder where she got this idea." Or "Kelly is going to tell us something she's learned about whales. Let's listen carefully to see if we should add this information to our class chart." Through words and actions the teacher guides the children toward active engaged listening.

This same type of engaged listening occurs during shared reading. The key to developing active engaged listeners is helping children to understand the expectation that they have a role in the shared reading experience, that the role of listener is vital to understanding the story. Teachers scaffold the initial listening experiences by focusing children's attention as they move through the text. Carefully phrased comments and questions such as "This part tells about his family. Listen, is it like your family?" guide children in their listening and help them to comprehend the story. To move children's attention to the sound and structure of the story, the teacher suggests that children listen to the sounds of the words. Invitations to listen to how beautiful these words are or listen for how the words rhyme scaffold the listening experience.

Listening Games

Another way to help children become active engaged listeners is through listening games. These have the very direct purpose of teaching young children to think about listening in an attentive, analytical way. Initially, the types of games children play require identification of sounds and the sources of sounds. As children become more proficient listeners, games challenge children to listen for sounds that are alike and sounds that are different. Children learn to identify rhyme, alliteration, syllables, words, and sentences through listening games. A variety of classroom games enhances listening skills and helps children to develop memory and the concept of sequence. A few examples of listening games follow.

This game helps children to focus on the sounds in their environment. Ask the children to sit in a circle. Have the children close their eyes, then ask them to identify the sounds they are hearing. The sounds used as a stimulus can be made in the classroom or recorded on audiotape. Sounds children identify can be sounds of the classroom (e.g., pencil sharpener, stapler, chalk on the chalkboard), sounds of home (e.g., baby crying, water running from faucets, footsteps on stairs, alarm clock ringing), outdoor sounds (e.g., wind blowing, snow crunching, rain falling, thunder rumbling), or sounds that students might expect to hear as part of a related area of study. Connecting the sounds being identified with units of study will provide a bridge to the classroom curriculum. After children have identified the sounds, ask them to think of other sounds that they might have heard at this location. Repeat this activity at other times with other stimulus sounds. Put the audiotapes in the listening center for the children to listen to at other times. Invite the children to draw pictures of the objects making the sounds.

Put a variety of objects that make noise (e.g., a bell, a whistle, a hammer, a stapler) into a mystery listening box. Ask the children to close their eyes. Invite one child to come to the box and choose an object. Have him or her use the object to make a sound, then allow that child to pick another child to identify the source of the sound. If that child guesses correctly, then he or she is the next to choose an object from the box. To extend children's listening ability, begin to have the children make more than one sound at a time. Ask the children to identify how many sounds they heard and what the sounds were.

Use drums to tap out rhythms. Have the children repeat the patterns heard. Increase the length and difficulty of the patterns over time. After children have become proficient at repeating the patterns, have them generate patterns for others to copy. This activity can also be done with clapping and makes an excellent activity for classroom transitions.

The children's song "Where, Oh, Where Has My Little Dog Gone?" is easily translated into a listening game. Children sit in a circle with their eyes closed while one child takes the role of the little dog and finds a hiding place in the classroom. The class sings a verse of the song and the little dog barks to help the children identify its hiding place. The children locate the little dog by pointing to and guessing the dogs location based on the barking sound.

Words and Syllables

One of the concepts that will be essential to the young reader is the word. Young children have only the vaguest notion of this concept. As children become phonologically aware, they develop a sensitivity to the units of speech. They become aware of words, syllables, and ultimately of individual phonemes. This awareness develops with time and experience. To a very young child, a word is the object. *Cat,* for example, is a soft furry animal with four legs and a tail that says meow. There is no conception that one could write the letters *c-a-t* as a representation for that furry animal or that *c-a-t* is a word. As children develop and come to understand that language is a representation for thoughts, actions, and objects, they may still have no firm notion of a word. The concept of word develops as children are learning to read and write. Their understanding of this concept will change with time and experience.

The concept of word is easily developed through classroom experiences in shared reading and shared writing in which the teacher creates a scaffold for learning it. One of the techniques the teacher can use to demonstrate the concept of word to children is to point to the words as they are being read during shared reading. This subtly draws the children's attention to the concept of word. When the children are invited to read along, the teacher will remind the children to read together by looking at the word while pointing to it with the pointer. Again, the teacher has scaffolded the concept of word. For more explicit instruction the teacher may ask a child to come to the big book and show other children a specific word. There are a variety of ways to do this. The teacher might ask the child to frame the word by cupping it with his or her hands. The teacher might provide the child with a paper frame to frame the word, give the child waxed string to outline the word, or even use a toy paddle with a space cut out of the center to frame the word. The teacher might also highlight a word with highlighter tape. All of these experiences help children to shape their concept of word. The teacher will also want to engage children in a conversation about the concept of word, leading children to explain how they know that a word is a word. The teacher will want to help the children understand the role of the white space in defining the concept of word. Leading the children to see that it is a letter, as in *I* or *a,* or a combination of letters surrounded by white space that makes a word may eliminate confusion over the terms *word* and *letter* for some children. Talk between and among students sometimes brings clarity to concepts that are difficult for children when they are explained in adult terms.

Another opportunity for developing the concept of word is shared writing. The teacher writes with the children, using specific language to alert them to the nature and operational definition of *word.* The teacher will ask children what word to write next and what should be done before writing the next word, allowing the children to define the need for space between words. By scaffolding shared experiences and giving children daily opportunities to write independently, the teacher helps children to develop the concept of word.

As children become phonologically aware, they are able to separate a stream of speech into individual words. To help children perceive the breaks in the flow of language, the teacher might play a game of asking the children to clap the words in a sentence. For example, when presented with the sentence "I see the clown," children would clap four times. This activity can help the teacher to assess the level of understanding that children have about the concept of word. Further lessons can then be planned on the basis of this assessment. This type of analysis is also useful in supporting children's independent writing. When young children are writing a sentence such as "I have a dog," clapping the words in the sentence before writing can be helpful as the child plans what to write. By clapping the words the child has established that he or she will write four words. Depending on the stage of writing development, clapping will also help the child to determine the individual phonemes that make up each word. The emergent writer uses this knowledge about words and sentences to monitor one's progress as one writes.

Another unit of speech that children become aware of as they are developing phonological awareness is the syllable. Interestingly, children seem to be able to identify syllables before they are able to identify words (Adams, 1990). Winner et al. (1991) found that young children develop an awareness of syllables without the support of instruction. By the end of kindergarten, most children are able to identify syllables, count syllables, and delete the initial syllable from a multisyllabic word (Liberman et al., 1974: Stanovich et al., 1984; Yopp, 1988). Syllables are meaningless units of speech but may be easier for young children to attend to because the individual sounds of syllables are impossible to separate acoustically. Teachers can help children to learn to identify syllables and the number of syllables in multisyllabic words by having children clap, snap, or tap the syllables in known words, especially their names, or familiar phrases. When children are having difficulty identifying syllables, the teacher can help them to feel the syllables by placing their hand under their chin as they say a word. Children can feel the jaw drop once for each syllable that is voiced. When identifying the number of syllables in a multisyllable word, children become aware that words are made up of smaller units of speech. This is an important insight as children move toward phonemic awareness.

Rhyme

Phonological awareness begins with the recognition of the similarities of sounds. Perhaps the easiest type of similarity for young children to recognize is rhyme. The ability to recognize rhyme develops early. Maclean et al. (1987) found that children as young as 3 years old had an awareness of rhyme. This awareness is focused on the structure of the word rather than the meaning. It is this attention to structure that makes rhyming such a valuable starting point for helping children to develop phonological awareness. As children play with rhyme they begin to understand how the phonemes in words can be manipulated by changing the onset to create similar words. This recognition is the beginning of phonemic awareness, which will facilitate reading acquisition.

Rhyming is not only easy for most young children to learn, it is also fun. Children like the way that rhyming words sound and the way the words feel as they roll around in their mouth. Playing with rhymes, identifying and generating rhymes, is treated like playing a game. Children like to hear rhymes read aloud and to recite rhymes. Rhymes are often written in rhythmic patterns, making them all the more appealing to young children. These conditions increase the likelihood that children will use the rhymes they know as they engage in free play and center activities, thus increasing their understanding of rhyme.

To learn about rhyme, children need a wide variety of literacy experiences involving rhyming words. By giving children many experiences with rhyming in a variety of learning contexts, the teacher builds sensitivity to the sounds of language. No one experience is prerequisite to another, but each experience builds on the previous one. The depth of experience is the foundation that is needed so that the child can tie the experiences, the practical knowledge, with the theoretical, the academic language and perceptions about phonology that underlie reading and reading instruction. These experiences allow the teacher to connect children's previous experiences with the new task of learning to read by drawing attention to the phonetic features of English.

Finger Plays, Songs, Poems, and Nursery Rhymes

Every day in every preschool and kindergarten classroom (and the primary grades, too) children should have some time to delight in language. These experiences are playful moments when children learn language for no other reason than that it's fun—and while it's fun, it is also foundational to reading success. Finger plays, or what Marc Brown (1987) calls play rhymes, are a great beginning. Finger plays are short rhythmic poems that involve not only sound but also movement, an ideal combination for very young children. Perhaps the first finger play we are exposed to is "Pat-a-cake, pat-a-cake." Mothers and babies engage in this rhyme beginning shortly after birth. Toddlers and preschoolers delight in rhymes such as "One, Two, Buckle My Shoe" that invite children to listen for the sound of language as they rhyme *two* and *shoe, four* and *door,* as well as to move little muscles as they pretend to buckle a shoe and knock on a door. Because they involve the whole child, finger plays are a great way to get and hold children's attention. This makes these rhymes perfect for teaching language structure as children transition from one activity to another in the classroom. Many teachers can be heard saying, "One, two, three, eyes on me," to which children respond, "One, two, eyes on you." More finger plays and rhymes can be found in Marc Brown's Play Rhymes (1987).

Young children love to sing. This makes songs an excellent way to introduce them to the sounds of language. Often, songs for young children focus on rhyme or other aspects of language. This focuses the child's attention on the sounds of the language rather than its meaning. Songs such as "A-Hunting We Will Go" and "Down by the Bay" not only build children's sensitivity to rhyme but create opportunities for children to manipulate language to create rhymes as they add new verses to the song. An excellent resource for songs that develop phonological awareness is *Oo-pples and Boo-noo-noos* by Hallie Kay Yopp and Ruth Helen Yopp (1997).

Poems and nursery rhymes have a place in every classroom. In preschool and kindergarten, poems and rhymes play a pivotal role in helping children to develop the understanding that they can examine language not only for its meaning but also for its structure. Through poems and nursery rhymes, adults let go and play with language and issue an invitation to children to do the same. A wonderful starting place for exploring rhyming words is the poem "Willoughby Wallaby Woo." This simple poem invites children to have fun with their own name and the names of their classmates, the perfect starting point for meaningful learning. "Willoughby Wallaby Wee, An elephant sat on me. Willoughby Wallaby Woo, An elephant sat on you," begins each child's examination of his or her own name and how it might sound if a rhyming word started with *w*; thus, *Daryl* becomes *Waryl* and *Jane* becomes *Wane*. This type of play with language requires children to be active participants in the construction of the concept of rhyme. Nursery rhymes like "Hickory, Dickory, Dock" and "To Market" invite children to create new verses with new rhyming words. Children should be encouraged to learn poems and rhymes and to create their own rhymes.

Another type of rhyme is the jump rope rhyme. Although these may not have the same impact on preschoolers, who are not yet be able to jump rope, they can have a tremendous impact on helping primary age children, who have not yet developed phonological awareness, to do so. Jump rope rhymes are rhythmic and often use nonsense words, which makes them perfect for changing children's focus from the meaning to the form of language. The teacher has an opportunity to tie a student's learning to something very meaningful by using jump rope rhymes to develop phonological awareness. An example of a jump rope rhyme would be "I went downtown to meet Mrs. Brown. She gave me a nickel, I bought a pickle. The pickle was sour, I bought a flower." The child who is jumping adds a new rhyme with each jump. For other examples of jump rope rhymes see *The Jump Rope Book* (Loredo, 1996).

Primary age children, who are often very involved in group games, also learn counting out rhymes. These rhymes, which are used to determine who will have the first turn, usually have a strong rhythm and often contain nonsense words. Like jump rope rhymes, they are of high interest to children. They are easy to learn and contain language that makes them perfect for developing concepts about language structure. "Engine, engine, number nine, coming down the railroad line. If the train should jump the track, would you get your money back? O-U-T spells out, and out goes you" is one example of a counting out rhyme.

Shared Reading and Read-Alouds

Poems and rhymes are a very direct way of helping children to understand rhyme, but much of what children come to understand about language and language structure comes from books and their interactions with adults around books. Many books that are perfect for shared reading and read-alouds help to develop phonological awareness, including rhyme. Books such as *"I Can't," Said the Ant* (Cameron, 1961), *Hop on Pop* (Seuss, 1965), and *"Buzz," Said the Bee* (Lewison, 1992) play with rhyme as the story develops. When reading stories that have rhyme, encourage children to identify the words that rhyme. Play with those words. Say them quickly. Say them slowly. Think of other words that rhyme with them. In a classroom setting, make lists of those words and post them in a poetry center or a writing center for children to use as they recite poetry or write new rhymes. Read these stories again and again. Repetition plays a role in the development of phonological awareness. A bibliography of books that facilitate the development of phonological awareness through rhyme can be found in Appendix A.

Assessing Phonological Awareness

Phonological awareness develops over time as children participate in a wide variety of literacy experiences. Unlike the acquisition of many other skills in reading, there isn't a moment when a child lacks phonological awareness and then suddenly becomes phonologically aware. The teacher will want to develop an ongoing record of the students' understanding of phonological awareness. Anecdotal records and class checklists will document this progress. We suggest that the teacher use both assessments to capture progress over time and the details of that progress. Figure 3-1 shows a class checklist. On this checklist the teacher charts the phonological awareness activities that have been planned for the whole class or groups of children in the class. Student names are listed along the left side of the paper. Across the top of the page, each lesson is dated and labeled with a title that briefly describes the instructional setting. The teacher marks the students' level of success with the lesson.

This type of assessment allows the teacher to evaluate the progress of the class at a glance. It is useful as a chronology of classroom instruction and student development. It is an effective tool in planning future lessons. Using what is known about the development of phonological awareness in young children and the instructional focus of the lessons previously taught, the teacher plans lessons that specifically meet the needs of this particular group of children. The checklist can be used to create groups to teach a specific skill or groups of children who are working with approximately the same level of expertise. This type of grouping is flexible, to allow the teacher to meet the many and various needs of the children in the class.

Anecdotal records provide the teacher with the rich details of each student's progress. Anecdotal records are dated observational notes that detail the child's

Figure 3-1. Class Checklist

Phonological Awareness Checklist E = emergent understanding D = developing understanding C = comprehensive understanding	identification of rhyming words Willoughby Wallaby Woo 9/27/98	rhyming words–picture sort 9/28/98	production of rhyming words shared reading 9/29/98	production of rhyming words Willoughby Wallaby Woo 9/30/98			
Alana	D	D	E	E			
Bethany	D	D	E	E			
David	C	C	D	C			
Gerald	E	E	E	E			
Isabella	E	D	E	E			
Juan	D	D	D	D			
Leon	D	D	E	E			
Melinda	E	E	E	E			
Nancy	D	D	E	D			

learning behaviors in both formal and informal settings. Part of the power of anecdotal records comes from allowing the teacher to capture unplanned, and sometimes unexpected, moments of student learning. Because there is no prescribed format, the teacher creates a record that exactly recalls the learning situation in a way that is useful to him or her. Many teachers develop their own shorthand for taking anecdotal records.

It is important that the anecdotal notes describe what the child is able to do, to allow the teacher to look for patterns of behavior. Notes such as "Emily produced a rhyming word for three during a class innovation on 'Hickory Dickory Dock'" has considerable more use than a note such as "Emily understands rhyming." The first note, when looked at with others, can help to develop a picture of Emily as a learner. The teacher can see that Emily not only recognizes rhymes in shared reading situations but can also produce rhymes in a shared writing lesson. This might lead the teacher to anticipate that Emily's understanding of rhyme has progressed so that future lessons should focus on helping Emily use this understanding to move toward learning segmentation of onsets and rimes. The onset of a word or syllable is the beginning letters before the vowel. The rime is the part of a word or syllable that begins with a vowel. The second entry leaves the reader wondering how one knows that Emily understands rhyming and what exactly is meant by "understands," since rhyming is a multifaceted concept. Figure 3-2 shows examples of anecdotal records.

Figure 3-2. Anecdotal Records

Name: *Allen* Date : *9-27* Context: *Circle time* *Allen's face lit up as I chanted Willoughby Wallaby Wallen. He couldn't wait to say his name. He was very quiet at the beginning but was offering answers by the end of the lesson.*	Name: *Jane* Date : *9-27* Context: *Housekeeping center* *"This is our baby. Her name is Willoughby Wallaby Wane. Just kidding. It's Jane, like me."*
Name: *Melinda* Date : *9-28* Context: *Pocket chart* *Lined picture cards up by categories, animals, toys, etc. No demonstration of rhyming.*	Name: *David* Date : *9-28* Context: *Pocket chart* *Quickly sorted the pict. into rhyming pairs. Worked in an orderly way, one pair at a time. Invited Tommy to play a game with the picture cards. Very engaged.*

Anecdotal records that document understanding of phonological awareness are taken during language games, shared reading, shared writing, writing workshop, and morning message. The teacher is likely to capture serendipitous demonstrations of understanding by recording children as they work in centers. The reading center, poetry center, alphabet center, block center, housekeeping center, and dramatic play center are all rich environments that encourage children to use language.

Anecdotal records can be taken on forms developed just for that purpose, like the example shown in Figure 3-2, or they can be taken on note cards, sticky notes, plain paper attached to a clipboard, or a quickly scrounged scrap of paper. All anecdotal records should be dated and give the context of the observation: Was it during shared reading, in the block center, or overheard while children were transitioning between activities? More important than the format or paper source is developing a way to organize the anecdotal records so that they are easily accessible and in a logical order. This is most often alphabetical by the students' first or last names. This can be done in hanging files, a notebook, or file folders. Developing a system for organization allows the teacher to review the records often. The ongoing review of assessment measures is the critical component in classrooms that provide instruction that meets the student at the edge of his or her capabilities and moves the student to new and deeper understandings.

CHAPTER 4

 Phonemic Awareness

One of the joys of teaching young children is watching their sense of playfulness with language develop. One of the indications of that playfulness is the day they discover the Name Game. With great delight, they turn from friend to friend and sing the Name Game song, substituting names as they go, and so you hear "Jane, Jane, bo bane, banana, banna, bo bane, fe, fi, fo fane, Jane" and "Ellen, Ellen, bo bellen, banana, banna, bo bellen, fe, fi, fo fellen, Ellen" as the group proceeds down the hallway to class. This ability to manipulate language is a sure indication that these children have developed phonemic awareness. Phonemic awareness is a part of phonological awareness. As mentioned in the previous chapter, phonemic awareness is a more complex level of phonological awareness and develops later in most children. *Phonemes* are the individual sound units of language. They are the single sounds that distinguish one word from another (Wilde, 1997). For example, *ran* and *can* differ by only one phoneme; similarly, *ran* and *run* differ by a single phoneme, and *ran* and *rat* differ by one phoneme. By manipulating a single sound, whether in the initial, medial, or final position, we create a different word. Phonemic awareness, the ability to identify and manipulate phonemes, develops with time, experience, and instruction.

It is important to understand what phonemic awareness is and also what it is not. Phonemic awareness is not phonics. Phonemes are the sounds of language. They are spoken. Children perceive phonemes through auditory channels. Phonics is the relationship between the phonemes, the sounds, and the letters of language. Children perceive phonics through auditory and visual channels. They hear the sound and see and understand that the sound is represented by a specific letter. During play, young children can sometimes be heard playing with language. They chant phrases such as, "I have a block, lock, tock, wock." They have no understanding that they are changing the initial letter of the words as they sing. They are aware only of the sound of the words. The child says *wock* because it is sound, not sense, that is the object of the play. As children become phonemically aware, they are quite probably also beginning to learn about phonics. They are beginning to learn about the letters that are related to the sounds they are making. The development of understandings about phonemic awareness and of phonics are related. As children talk, sing, and play language games in the classroom, they are developing a deeper understanding of phonemic awareness and often an understanding of phonics. It is possible to separate the two for purposes of discussion, but in classroom practice the development of phonemic awareness and of phonics often occur simultaneously.

Development of Phonemic Awareness

Awareness of phonemes can be demonstrated across a continuum of tasks. At one end of the continuum are the tasks that require recognition of rhyme, identifying *chick* and *stick* as rhyming words, and production of rhyme, responding with *chick* when prompted with *stick*. These are followed by oddity tasks. Oddity tasks require identification of words that begin or end with the same phoneme when presented in a series of words, some of which do not begin or end with the same phoneme. For example, when prompted with *chick, ship,* and *cheese,* the child responds *chick* and *cheese.* More difficult than oddity tasks are tasks that require blending individual phonemes into words. These require the understanding that phonemes are units of sound. That a unit of sound smaller than the word or syllable exists is a high-level insight for young children. The tasks also require the understanding that by blending phonemes together one can produce a meaningful word. An example would be to blend *ch, i, k* to produce *chick.* This insight, or the lack of it, may be foundational to the difficulties many children have with stretching through a word or sounding a word out when problem solving unknown words. Another task that is similarly difficult is phoneme deletion, or what Adams (1990) refers to as syllable-splitting. In these tasks individuals are presented with a prompt, such as *chick,* and are asked either to articulate the initial phoneme *ch* or to remove the initial phoneme and articulate the remaining sounds *ick.* Further along on the continuum is phoneme segmentation. One is asked to analyze a given word into its constituent phonemes; thus *chick* becomes *ch, i, k.* The most complex tasks on the continuum require not only segmentation of the word into its individual phonemes but also manipulation of the phonemes by adding, deleting, or moving one of the phonemes to another location. As an example, children might be asked to change the *i* in *chick* to *e*, resulting in *check*, or the *ch* in *chick* to *s,* resulting in *sick.*

Although children's ability to rhyme, match, blend, delete, segment, and manipulate phonemes exists on a continuum of difficulty, like much of child development, progression across the continuum is seldom smooth or evenly paced. Children may exhibit different levels of ability across several tasks at the same time. It is also true that some children become very proficient at identifying alliterative sounds or performing oddity tasks before they are proficient at identifying rhyming pairs, a task generally considered to be easier for most children to complete successfully. Accommodating for the individual differences in students and providing opportunities for children to develop phonemic awareness abilities on a variety of tasks across the continuum of development is fundamental to well-planned classroom instruction.

The importance of phonemic awareness to success in reading is generally agreed upon by reading educators. Phonemic awareness plays a critical role in the development of the ability to decode words and read for meaning (Adams, 1990; Juel, 1988, 1991). Children enter our classrooms at various places on the continuum of phonemic awareness development. Some children will enter with little or no sense of phonemic awareness, whereas others will be able to manipulate phonemes with speed and accuracy. The classroom teacher will be asked to ensure that all children are phonemically aware as quickly as possible. In doing so, the teacher needs to ensure that the instruction children receive is appropriate for their age and development, builds on what children know as they develop new understandings about phonemes and how to manipulate them, and maintains the playful nature of learning about language. This instruction includes rhymes, games, and songs. Children should have daily opportunities to investigate phonemic awareness as they engage in reading and writing activities. The teacher weaves opportunities to model and explore phonemic awareness into these activities. There is evidence to indicate that 80% to 85% of children develop phonemic awareness by the middle of first grade as a result of typical experiences at home and school (Allington, 1997). The quality of children's instructional experiences and their relationship to reading and writing have a significant impact on the rate of development and lasting effects of phonemic awareness acquisition.

The development of phonemic awareness is a long process that is very much influenced by the opportunities a child has to explore language. Children who have opportunities to listen to language, to discuss language with others, and to play with language are likely to develop phonemic awareness with effective classroom instruction. Classrooms that promote the development of phonemic awareness provide children with these opportunities. Children are given time, materials, and the necessary support to listen to language, talk about language, and play with language. The teacher helps children to develop phonemic awareness in planned instructional settings such as shared reading, shared writing, and interactive writing. The teacher creates a classroom environment that supports children as they work at becoming phonemically aware by provisioning the environment with materials that invite children to explore the sounds of language. Finally, the teacher builds into the day multiple opportunities for children to develop phonemic awareness in independent settings.

Teacher Talk

Young children are very much influenced by the enthusiasms of their teacher. Some classes avidly follow Alaskan dogsled races because the teacher has an interest in the Iditarod; others become young oceanographers because the teacher has an interest in deep sea diving. This same enthusiasm and interest can also be shared when we are talking about language. Language is an amazing invention. Seeing how all the parts fit together, how language works, can be fascinating for young children. It is an extraordinary puzzle. The approach we take to helping children learn about language may determine their enthusiasm for that learning and ultimately their ability to learn. How teachers talk about language, their interest and wonder about language, their joy and playfulness with language, influences how children approach the task of learning language. Teacher talk is very powerful as a way of helping children to develop phonemic awareness. The teacher needs to talk about language and point out to children how language works, how language sounds, and how language changes, separate from the meaning that language conveys. This talk should be part of the ongoing conversations the teacher has with children around reading and writing. While reading *Solo Plus One* (Scamell, 1992)*,* the story of a cat who has a fancy for duck eggs, the teacher draws children's attention to the author's word choice of *wriggled, snuggled,* and *waggled.* The children are asked to listen to the words, say the words, let them roll around in their mouths. They talk about how the words are alike. The focus is on the sound of language. When reading Pat Hutchins' (1989) delightful *Don't Forget the Bacon,* in which the little boy is trying to remember a shopping list and "six farm eggs" becomes "six fat legs" and then "six clothes pegs," the teacher has the perfect opportunity to talk about language manipulation and to give children the opportunity to play with language. As the teacher writes with children, he or she talks about how to say the word slowly, how to segment the word so they can hear the sounds in the word. They talk about how to add a part to a word to change the word so that it shows something that happened in the past. They explore language and look for ways to make connections to things the children knew previously while moving them toward discovering new things.

Games and Songs

Games and songs are particularly suited to helping children learn about language because of the age and developmental level of the children we are teaching. Certainly the concepts in phonemic awareness could be developed in a very didactic manner, but this would be inappropriate, especially for those we are trying to help most, the children who have had little opportunity to develop phonemic awareness skills prior to coming to school. Games and songs are also important because, for those children who are less phonemically aware, games and songs are often part of their home experience prior to school. This makes a link between the things valued at home and the things valued at school.

As children become phonemically aware, they will explore playing with sounds that rhyme, sounds that match, sounds that can be blended, sounds that are deleted from words and syllables, sounds that are segmented, and sounds that are manipulated. Games and songs that help children to develop the ability to recognize and produce rhymes were discussed in the previous chapter. In this section, games and songs that develop abilities on the remaining phonemic awareness tasks will be discussed.

Sound Matching

Young children understand language primarily as a whole, as meaningful units. When children begin to develop phonemic awareness, they must recognize the units of speech smaller than the word or syllable. A first step in this process is helping children to hear the similarities in words. The similarities at the beginning of words are the easiest to discriminate and should be focused on first. Later, children can distinguish how words are alike in medial and final positions as well. Singing songs and playing games in which children are asked to match sounds or to sort sounds develop this initial acknowledgment of phonemes.

Begin with familiar children's songs and turn the focus of the children to language. As an example, children might sing "Mary Had a Little Lamb." Then, begin changing the song to include names of the children in the class and matching the initial phoneme of the child's name with an animal and an action. Children might sing verses like the following:

> Tara had a tiny turtle,
> Tiny turtle, tiny turtle,
> Tara had a tiny turtle,
> That was green and tough.

or

> Kiera had a cuddly cat,
> Cuddly cat, cuddly cat,
> Kiera had a cuddly cat,
> That was quiet and cute.

The verse can be followed by a refrain:

> Can you name a /k/ word,
> A /k/ word, a /k/ word?
> Can you name a /k/ word?
> Tell us your /k/ word now.

Songs like this focus children's attention on the initial phoneme of words. Later, as children become proficient in letter-sound identification, they will notice that Kiera and cat begin with different letters. This presents an excellent opportunity to discuss the fact that in English the same phoneme is represented by more than one letter. The teacher should never shy away from exploring language because it doesn't follow the rules. It is these anomalies that make English such an interesting and rich language.

Innovations on familiar nursery rhymes also create wonderful opportunities for children to match sounds. Using the Mother Goose rhyme "To Market," ask children to listen for a specific phoneme and then to produce a word that begins with a matching phoneme. The teacher creates a new verse for the poem, such as the following:

> To market, to market,
> To buy a brown bug,
> Home again, home again,
> Jiggity jug.

Then children are asked to produce the name of something they will buy that begins with the same phoneme:

> To market, to market,
> What did you buy,
> That begins with /b/?
> Tell us, please try.

All children should have a turn adding something to the list. The game goes on for as long as the teacher can think of alliterative prompts for getting the children started and the children are interested in playing.

There are a variety of games that help children to develop the ability to match sounds. The teacher will want to consider any game that gives children the opportunity to listen to sounds in words and that allows the child to demonstrate the ability to discriminate or produce a matching sound. One way this might be accomplished is to give children some type of special signal for responding to oral prompts. For example, the teacher might attach bright sparkling stars to wooden sticks (large colorful happy faces on cards also work) and give these to children to use when responding. Explain to the children that they are going to play a listening game. Give each child a star. Tell the children that they are going to listen for the *t* sound at the end of words. Whenever the teacher says a word that ends with the target sound, the children are to hold up the star. A quick visual check of the children's responses tells the teacher which children are able to hear the sound and which children will need additional help. Children can be asked to listen for a sound at the beginning, middle, or end of the word.

A very familiar game, *I Spy*, can be adapted for sound matching. The teacher prompts children with the chant, "I spy with my little eye something that starts with /h/." Children then try to identify something that begins with a matching phoneme. The game continues with other phonemes. The scope of the game can be changed by limiting the number of phonemes the children are asked to match, the position of the matching phoneme (children could be asked to spy something that ends with a matching phoneme), or the places in which children look for an object containing the matching phoneme. Children can look for objects in the environment or they can search illustrations in books.

When playing *I Spy*, children begin with a phoneme and search for an object that contains a matching phoneme. In the game *Mystery Sound*, children are prompted with objects and asked to identify the common phoneme. The teacher places a variety of objects containing the same phoneme in a mystery bag. The target phoneme might be at the beginning, middle, or end of the word. The teacher tells the children where to listen for the sound. She might ask children to listen for the same sound in the middle of each word. Children are asked to reach into the bag and pull out an object. The child says the name of the object, listens for the sound, and places the object on a work space. Each child is given a turn. The children repeat the name of all of the objects, listening carefully for the matching phoneme, until several objects have been taken from the bag. Children are then given the opportunity to identify the sound.

Sound Blending

As children develop a basic understanding of phonemes, they recognize them as small units of sound and begin to develop the concept that a phoneme might be found at the beginning, middle, or end of a word. They will also need to understand that by blending phonemes together they can create words. Children learn this in a variety of ways, but songs and games are especially effective. Blending is not a concept where telling children what you want them to do will prove effective. Children need the opportunity to try it out. They need to play with words and blend the sounds together so that their tongue feels the sounds, their ears hear the sounds, and often so they experience the word kinesthetically as well. Blending activities may be easier for children if they are initially done with onsets and rimes.

After children have learned the song "The Muffin Man," the teacher will teach children the following verse:

> Oh, do you know the word I say,
> The word I say, the word I say?
> Oh, do you know the word I say?
> It sounds like this…

At the end of the verse the teacher will prompt children with a segmented word. For example, the teacher might say, "It sounds like this, /d/, /u/, /k/."The word can be segmented into onset and rime or individual phonemes, depending on the needs of the children.

Children will respond by singing the following verse and supplying the blended word:

> Oh yes, we know the word you said,
> The word you said, the word you said.
> Oh yes, we know the word you said,
> The word you said was…

For the example given, the children would respond with *duck*.

Nursery rhymes, with just a few innovations, offer children opportunities to blend phonemes. One of the rhymes that works for this is "Old King Cole." The teacher repeats the verse and changes the last line to substitute a segmented word in place of the original phrase.

> Old King Cole was a merry old soul,
> A merry old soul was he,
> He called for his pipe and he called for his bowl,
> And he called for his */l/-/a/-/m/*.

Children blend the segmented word to decide what the king has called for, in this case a *lamb*.

Another nursery rhyme that will work for blending is "Handy Spandy." The last line of the rhyme is changed into a question and a segmented response. Children blend the segmented word together to determine the answer to the question.

> Handy spandy, sugary candy,
> French almond rock;
> Butter and bread for your supper,
> What have you got?
> I've got */p/-/l/-/u/-/m/-/z/*.

Many young children learn best when they are physically involved in a task. To involve children in blending phonemes into words, have them use rhythm sticks or drums to tap the phonemes and blended word, or clap the onset, rime, and blended word. Children repeat */m/, /a/, /n/, man*, while tapping four times, or they repeat */m/, /an/, man* while clapping three times.

Another way to give children practice blending words is to have them listen to robot talk and help the robot to talk as we do by telling it the name of the object the robot is looking at. The robot says a little rhyme:

> I am a robot.
> Can you help me?
> Can you tell me what I see?
> I see a */k/-/a/-/t/*.

The children then respond by blending the segmented word to produce the answer, in this case *cat*.

Phoneme Deletion

As children become adept at identifying matching phonemes, they are capable of examining words by deleting the initial consonant sound. Deleting this sound not only changes the sound of the word but in some cases results in a new word with an entirely different meaning.

Help children to become word magicians. Introduce this game by telling the children that they are going to learn to do a magic trick. They are going to turn one word into another by removing one of the sounds. Give an example by saying, "Watch me magically change this word into an entirely new word. I start with cup, *k-k-k-up* and take away the *k*, and *abra cadabra*, I have… [pause for effect and thinking]. Can anyone tell me? That's right, I have *up*." Continue with other phoneme deletions. Select the words for phoneme deletions from words that contain familiar phonograms such as *–at, –an, –and, –it, –old, –end, –eat, –ice, –ill, –ow*, and *–in*.

This same magic trick can be done in reverse when children are learning to manipulate sounds. Children are told a word and asked to add a phoneme to make a new word.

To give children practice identifying the onsets of words, play a game of *What's Left?* The teacher and children sit in a circle on the floor. The teacher asks a question that requires the child to delete the rime from a known word. For example, what's mouse without the *ouse*? The teacher then rolls a rubber ball to one of the children. The child answers, "Mouse without the *ouse* is *m*." The child then rolls the ball back to the teacher. The game is repeated for as long as time permits and children are interested in playing. The game can also be played by deleting the onset and letting children identify the rime.

Segmenting Phonemes

As children become more phonemically aware, they are able to recognize and segment all of the phonemes in regularly spelled words. Initially, as children attempt to segment words, it can be helpful to provide them with visual or manipulative support. One way to do this is to give children linking cubes and have them break apart the cube as they segment the word. To segment the word bat the child is given three cubes and breaks off a cube while verbalizing each phoneme, *b, a, t.*

Another way to involve the whole child in the task of segmentation is to give children a large rubber ball and have them bounce the ball one time for each phoneme in a word. The teacher says *pie* and the children bounce their ball twice, once for each phoneme as they segment the word. Children might also hop or jump as they verbalize the phonemes.

Have the children sing "Old McDonald Had a Farm." When the children get to the part where they name an animal, have them say the name by segmenting it. The other children demonstrate that they have understood the word by responding with the appropriate animal sound.

Sound Manipulation

At the far end of the continuum of phonemic awareness tasks are those that require children to manipulate the sounds in the words. This manipulation can range from fairly simple to very complex. A task that might be considered relatively easy would involve changing a known word to a new word by changing the initial phoneme. Children might be asked to change the *b* in *bat* to *s* and tell the new word, *sat*. At the more complex end of these tasks would be an activity like the Name Game, where the same phoneme is being changed across several nonsense words.

There are several delightful children's songs that are based on this concept. *Oo-pples and Boo-noo-noos: Song and Activities for Phonemic Awareness* by Hallie Yopp and Ruth Yopp (1997) is a good resource for these songs. Familiar songs with nonsense lyrics, like "Zippity-Doo-Dah," "This Old Man," and "Row, Row, Row Your Boat" all have familiar refrains that can be changed by manipulating the initial phoneme. *Zippity-doo-dah* becomes *hippity-hoo-hah*, *knick-knack-paddy-wack* becomes *mick-mack-daddy-sack*, and *merrily, merrily, merrily* becomes *berrily, berrily, berrily* as children play with and manipulate phonemes.

Shared Reading

Shared reading is most often thought of as an activity that develops reading skills for decoding and comprehension, but the teacher can also help children to develop phonemic awareness by drawing children's attention to the sound patterns in the text. For example, when reading *A, My Name Is Alice* by Jane Bayer (1984), the intent of the story is the playful exploration of alliteration. The teacher first uses this as an opportunity for children to listen for the repeating phoneme; later, after rereading the book, it becomes an opportunity for children to produce alliterative phrases as they use their own names to innovate on the text. Children take turns creating verses such as "K, my name is Kate. My husband's name is Ken. We come from Kansas and we sell kangaroos."

The exploration of phonemic awareness begins with a phrase or refrain from the text, then children move away from the text to play with the sounds of the language before making something that belongs uniquely to them and demonstrates their understanding of phonemic awareness. Phrases like those in Bruce Degen's (1990) *Jamberry*, such as "Rumble and ramble, In blackberry bramble, Billions of berries, For blackberry jamble," implore children to play with language until they produce "Red cherries, Black cherries, Cherries that are yummy, Cherries for my tongue and cherries for my tummy!"

Some books demand that we attend to the sounds of the language as much as the message in the story. Such a story is *Two Cool Cows* by Toby Speed (1995). This story of two cows and their trip to the moon plays with language in so many ways that it is a delight to any reader. The teacher encourages children to listen and linger over the language of the text. From the very first page, where we find "the hills of Hillimadoon and Willimadoon and Rattamadoon and Hattamadeen," to the end of the adventure, with "Cows, kids, buttons, boots, back to the Huckabuck Farm," there are opportunities to talk to children about sounds that rhyme, sounds that are the same, sounds that are changed, and sounds that can be manipulated.

Sound Sorts

Well before children are ready to learn letter-sound relationships in any formal manner, they are able to hear and discriminate between phonemes at the beginning of words. To help children develop this ability, the teacher looks for ways that children can sort by sound. In the classroom, this takes the form of oral language games, or it can be accomplished by having children sort objects or pictures of objects. Collections of real objects are placed in a bucket, box, or basket, and children are asked to sort the objects into groups according to the beginning sound. It is important to keep in mind that at this point children are listening for the beginning phoneme, not trying to identify the beginning letter of the object. This means that children might find *cat* and *kangaroo* in the same sort because they begin with the same phoneme. Children are given a work mat with two large circles drawn on it, a variety of objects to be sorted, and a single object that represents the phonemes you wish children to listen for placed in the center of each circle. As an example, the teacher might give two students a bucket that contains a toy ball, bunny, fish, fly, boat, fox, butterfly, baby, fire truck, four, frog, bug, button, banana, five, bat, and bottle. In the center of one circle on the work mat, the teacher places a toy bear; in the center of the other circle, a toy fork. The children work together to place the other toys in the appropriate circle. It is much more powerful for children to work on this as a shared activity than to work on it independently. When children work together they talk to each other, saying the names of the objects they are identifying aloud many times. This gives children more opportunity to listen for the phoneme and provides them with a way to check their perceptions against those of another child. When children are first learning to sort by phoneme, all objects should begin with the phonemes the children are listening for. As children become more able, a few objects that do not begin with the same initial phoneme can be added. Children place these at the edge of the work mat. This makes the activity more challenging. When children have developed some facility at sorting by phoneme, they can sort objects that begin with three or more different phonemes at the same time. Children can also be asked to listen for and sort objects according to ending or middle sounds.

The same skill can be developed using picture cards. Sets of picture cards are available commercially, but the teacher can draw, cut from magazines, or use clip art to create her own sets of picture cards. When making sets of picture cards, it is a wonderful idea to include cards with photos of the children on them. Children's names are very meaningful, and this can increase the power of the activity enormously. Children sort the picture cards into piles or use a pocket chart for sorting the pictures. Place a picture of an object beginning with one target phoneme on the left side of the pocket chart and a picture of an object beginning with the other phoneme on the right side of the pocket chart, then give the children a stack of picture cards and have them place the cards in the chart under the matching picture. As the children become more adept at listening for phonemes, sort three or more sounds or listen for the sounds in other positions in the word.

Say It Like a Snail

One of the tasks children must learn if they are to develop phonemic awareness is the segmentation of the individual phonemes in words. To do this successfully, they must slow down their processing of each syllable enough to distinguish the individual sounds in a seemingly indivisible unit. In order for children to do this quickly, they need a large amount of practice saying words slowly. One way the teacher helps children to accomplish this goal is to create a playful setting in which children can practice. Teaching children to say it like a snail is such a setting. Ask children how they think a snail might talk. Discuss the fact that snails move very slowly and pose the notion that snails talk the same way. Once the children have the idea that snails talk very slowly, demonstrate how a snail might say *cat* or *dog* or other words with which the children are very familiar. Practice having the children identify a few words, then give them the opportunity to say it like a snail. Play the game often. Games need only last for a few minutes. When asking children to line up, call them to line by saying their names at snail speed. Designate one recess a week for snail speak and have children speak to each other and you at snail speed. Talking like a snail gives children practice segmenting phonemes as they make their wants and needs known and practice blending phonemes as they listen to others. There are any number of variations of this activity that the teacher might use with young children to help them develop the notion of segmenting phonemes.

Sound Boxes

Another technique for helping children to develop phonemic awareness is the use of sound boxes or Elkonin boxes. Young children approach the use of these boxes in a very playful way. The child is shown a picture of a familiar object—for example, an ape or a bee (see Figure 4-1). Under each picture are boxes, the number of which correspond to the number of speech sounds or phonemes in the word. For the word *ape* there are two boxes. The child is given counters and asked to push the counters into the boxes as they articulate the individual phonemes in the word. The child pushes one counter in the box while saying *a* and the second counter in the next box while saying *p*. This task is easier when the sounds are distinctly separate, as in *ape,* and difficult when the sounds of the syllable are acoustically inseparable, as in *bee*. We are asking the child to create the separation. The ability to hear and distinguish the phonemes comes about with experience and, for most children, the support of instruction.

When you are using sound boxes it is best to begin with words of two phonemes, such as *egg, tie,* or *ice*. As children become proficient with two-phoneme words, introduce words of three phonemes, such as *duck, light,* and *mug*. Once children find working with three phonemes easy, they can move on to words of four and five phonemes. When you are using sound boxes for the first time, the activity should be modeled for children. The teacher may want to play side-by-side with the child as the activity is introduced. Not all children will be ready for

Figure 4-1. Elkonin Boxes

this activity at the same time. Working with individuals and small groups will provide for the developmental needs of children better than whole-group lessons. Initially, sound boxes are for sounds; there is no expectation that children will match the sounds with letters. As children become competent with the boxes, and their knowledge of letter names and sound associations increases, the sound boxes may become a tool to facilitate spelling.

Invented Spelling

Invented spelling refers to beginners' use of the symbols children associate with the sounds they hear in the words they wish to write (Bredekamp, 1998). Writing with invented spelling shows what children understand about the translation of the sounds of language into print. Research has demonstrated that even the writing of three- and four-year-olds reflect phonetic and phonological analysis of speech (Chomsky, 1975; Read, 1971). Invented spelling, also called temporary spelling or phonic spelling, plays a significant role in the acquisition of phonemic awareness in young children. When children use invented spelling, they are engaging in the phonological analysis of the word they are attempting to write. Children analyze the word to determine how many sounds they hear, what sounds they hear, and in what order they hear these sounds. This analysis is the bridge from phonemic awareness to phonics. By examining a child's invented spelling, the teacher has an indication of the depth of the child's understanding of phonemic awareness. Children's early writing shows the abstractions they are making about the writing system of their culture (Snow, et al., 1998). Children begin by writing the initial sound of a word; soon their writing shows evidence of consonant frameworks, and later inclusion of vowels. Invented spelling is evidence of children's developing phonemic awareness. Children should be encouraged to write daily as part of a balanced language arts program. Use of invented spelling in their writing encourages the development of phoneme identity, phoneme segmentation, and phonics.

Shared Writing

When the teacher and children are writing together, the possibilities for instruction are endless. The teacher is given the opportunity to model the skills and strategies that literate individuals use for creating text. One of the skills writers use is the application of phonemic awareness as they encode words. The teacher demonstrates this process on selected words. When emergent writers attempt to write an unfamiliar word, they often vocalize the word as they write. The child segments the word being written into individual phonemes. The teacher models this process by asking children to say the word slowly. Often, the teacher will slightly exaggerate the spaces between phonemes to support children as they make initial attempts to divide syllabic units. After saying the entire word slowly, the teacher writes the letter representations for the phonemes the children have identified.

The teacher may also use what children know about the sounds of words to help them write unfamiliar words. When children are familiar with a phonogram as part of a word, the teacher calls on the children to apply this knowledge to a new word. For example, if the teacher knows the children are familiar with the word *car* and wish to use the word *star* in a class story, the teacher will ask the children if they know a word that sounds like *star*. The children are asked to apply their ability to produce a rhyme. When children identify the word *car*, the teacher asks the children which part of the words is alike. This requires the children to split the syllable and compare both the onsets and rimes. When the children identify the rime *-ar*, the teacher writes the rime on the board. Under the *-ar* the teacher writes *car*. The children listen to the phonogram and the word they know. Then the teacher works with the children to use the phonogram to write *star*. They work together to segment the *s* and *t*, then the phonogram *-ar* is written. This type of analysis and application is a significant part of any shared writing experience and draws on what children know about phonemic awareness and phonics.

Independent Writing

Perhaps the best activity for helping children to develop phonemic awareness is independent writing. As children write, they translate the word they are writing to the phonemes that make up the word. An examination of the writing of young children shows evidence of the number of phonemes the child hears in a word and the order in which they hear these phonemes. Recent research by Vernon and Ferreiro (1999) found that phonemic awareness is related to the acquisition of an alphabetic writing system. In the following writing sample (Figure 4-2), Sammy, a kindergarten student, is writing about his make-believe animal.

The animal is a cheetah that can fly. He writes, "Cheetahs can run fast and can fly too and his name is Justin." Sammy's understanding of the alphabetic principle and awareness of phonemes is apparent. He is able to hear the initial

Figure 4-2. Writing Sample No. 1

phoneme in each word. Through instruction he has learned that the *ch* sound is represented by two letters, and he treats the letters as if they were one. Notice that in *cheetah* he hears the initial sound in each syllable. Young children develop an awareness of syllables early (Winner et al., 1991), and this is reflected in Sammy's writing. After Sammy had written "cheetahs can run," the teacher dropped in on Sammy to see if help was needed. She noted his use of initial sounds and began to help him stretch to hear more of the phonemes in the words. With support, Sammy was able to hear both the initial and the final consonant sound as evidenced by the word *can,* written as *c* independently and as *cn* with support from the teacher. Daily independent writing, beginning in kindergarten or as soon as children show an interest in writing, makes a significant contribution to the development of phonemic awareness, phonics, and reading. According to Vernon and Ferreiro (1999), if teachers encourage children to write and reflect on their writing, analysis of speech will take place.

Assessment of Phonemic Awareness

Although many factors account for children's eventual success as readers, their awareness of the phonemic structure of spoken words is one of the strongest predictors of success in reading (Adams, 1990). For this reason, it is important for the teacher to assess the developing phonemic awareness abilities of their students on an ongoing basis. Assessment and evaluation allows the teacher to develop lessons that support students as they move across the continuum of phonemic awareness tasks. This cyclical process of assessment, evaluation, and instruction provides direct instruction on those aspects of phonemic awareness most appropriate for the learning needs of each individual and for groupings of students in the class. At the same time, the teacher provides this instruction in meaningful contexts to ensure that the learning is connected to its function in learning to read and write. Children are learning about phonemic awareness and becoming phonemically aware as they are learning to read and write. Research has shown a reciprocal relationship between the ability to segment phonemes and literacy development (Lie, 1991; Perfetti et al., 1987; Winner et al., 1991).

Assessment of phonemic awareness is done in formal and informal settings. Each time children are engaged in phonemic awareness activities, the teacher has the opportunity to assess the development of phonemic awareness of the members of the group. Recording student responses on anecdotal records or checklists yields a picture of what children currently understand and are able to do. (See Figures 3-1 and 3-2.) Often the teacher is engaged in facilitating the activity, but an instructional assistant is available to make notes of student behavior. The teacher and instructional assistant discuss the observations and share insights about the progress of the children. Many types of games, songs, and play allow the teacher to be an outside observer. This is a perfect opportunity to listen for and record the development of phonemic awareness. Focused observations as children sort pictures by sounds at the pocket chart, retell nursery rhymes at the flannel board, say things like *snails* as they work in the block center, or play alliteration lotto in the games center provide information about the independent level of understanding of the children.

The teacher can obtain more formal assessment information by devising a series of tasks that demonstrate what children understand about rhyming, alliteration, syllables, blending, segmenting, and manipulating phonemes in words and administering the assessment in small-group or one-to-one settings. Experience has shown that these assessments validate what the teacher has observed in other instructional settings.

Additionally, student work samples, specifically journal or independent writing, demonstrate understanding of phonemic awareness and phonics. In writing samples, the teacher has a graphic demonstration of what the child hears and how that perception is translated into print. The teacher analyzes the writing sample and records the phonemes the child hears and the order in which the child hears the phonemes. The teacher also notes whether the child hears initial consonants, consonant frameworks, or all of the phonemes in a word. Additionally, the teacher will note when the child has begun to use conventional spelling. Figure 4-3 shows one child's writing sample and the teacher's notes on phonemic awareness and phonics.

Figure 4-3. Writing Sample No. 2

Writing samples are a valuable tool for recording the development of phonemic awareness and phonics, but the teacher may also want to know if children hear sounds that do not appear in student writing. To ensure that the teacher has a complete picture of what students know about phonemes, a dictation task that asks children to write a specific sentence may be used. Clay (1993a) devised a dictation task as part of a survey of early literacy behaviors. A dictation task shows what phonemes the child is able to hear and how the child represents those phonemes in print. The dictation task may be a sentence or a series of words. Figure 4-4 shows one child's development on a series of words across a school year. This list of words represents the sound-letter relationships and word-spelling patterns that the teacher felt were important for children in first grade to know. The assessment is administered several times each year, usually at the end of each academic quarter. This sample shown shows one child's understanding in September, January, and June. It is important to note that the list is not formally taught but is used as a gauge of the learning environment in which the children are immersed. Children are developing the ability to hear and represent sounds in words through talk, songs, games, reading, and writing experiences, as well as planned direct instruction based on the assessment and evaluation of student work.

Phonemic Awareness and Phonics

The line between phonemic awareness and phonics is often very hard to determine. Phonemic awareness is the awareness of the sounds that make up spoken words, and phonics is the understanding of which letters represent those sounds in writing, the sound-symbol relationship. Phonemic awareness is the structure that supports phonics and its application in reading, but it is not prerequisite to

Figure 4-4. Dictation Task

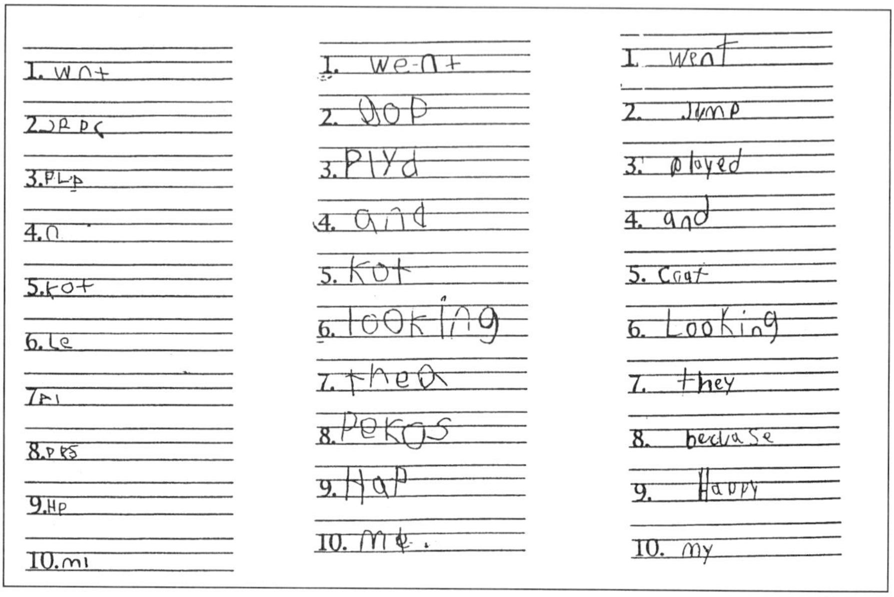

phonics. There is evidence of a reciprocal relationship between phonemic awareness and phonics. It appears that children benefit from some phonemic awareness activities prior to learning about letters and sounds. Once children know a little about phonemic awareness, it is important to learn about sounds and letters as they are learning about their application in reading and writing. Training children in phonemic awareness produces little reading benefit unless the children are also taught the letters each phoneme represents (Bradley & Bryant, 1983). Children need to make the connection between sounds, letters, and reading from their initial experiences with print. The activities in this chapter have focused on phonemes, on sounds. As the activities are introduced and children develop some awareness of the sounds, the teacher begins to introduce the letters the sounds are represented by and the purpose for knowing the sound-letter relationship—reading and writing. Understanding sounds and letters facilitates word recognition. Fast, fluent word recognition allows the reader to focus more cognitive energy on understanding the meaning of the text. Phonics and phonemic awareness are tools that allow the reader to focus on the goal of reading, understanding the author's message.

CHAPTER 5

 Teaching the Alphabet

One of the most memorable moments for many parents is the day their child stands in front of them and sings the A B C song from beginning to end. Intuitively, parents understand the importance of learning the alphabet to reading. The child is invited to display competence by singing the alphabet song for every available audience: the friend who drops by for coffee, grandma calling to say hello, and the neighbor who drives the preschool car pool. Even though singing this little song is only a first step in knowing the alphabet, it is a critical first step and for many parents an occasion for family celebration. As children develop as readers, they learn the alphabet in a variety of ways. They are able to identify upper- and lower-case letters, recognizing the distinguishable features of each. They are able to identify the sound one expects to hear when they see a given letter and a corresponding letter when prompted with a sound. These are all very different understandings about the alphabet. These understandings are far more sophisticated than the recitation of the alphabet song, and they develop over time as the result of experiences with the alphabet in the context of environmental print, books, games, and hands-on experiences. Some of the understandings about the alphabet that children must develop are the following:

- Every letter of the alphabet has a name.
- The name of the letter is always the same, but the shape of the letter may vary depending on the font and case.
- Each letter has distinctive features. The letter is determined by the spatial orientation and the size of the features.
- Each letter has an upper case and a lower case.

- Letters and numbers are different symbol systems.
- There is an order to the letters of the alphabet.
- The letters represent sounds.
- Some letters represent more than one sound.
- Some letters combine to represent a single sound.
- The letters can be combined to form words.

From playing with magnetic letters on the refrigerator door to singing the alphabet song, young children are fascinated with the alphabet. As early as 2 years of age, parents begin to draw their child's attention to the letters that he or she finds important, most often the letters of the child's name. The rapid and flexible identification of the letters of the alphabet is a foundational part of learning to read. Frequently, once children are able to recite the names of the letters, parents take an active role in helping them to identify the features that distinguish one letter from another. This is no easy task when one considers that **g**, g, g, *g*, *g*, **g**, *g*, and **g** are all the same letter but **q** is an entirely different letter. Research indicates that children learn letters by attention to interrelated sets of visual features and that with time and experience with a variety of print, children add spatial relationships to the sets of features that distinguish one letter from another, allowing them to determine that **p** and **q** are entirely different letters (Gibson, 1969). Children need a rich variety of experiences with print to become sensitive to letter shapes, names, and sounds.

When children sing the alphabet song, they are learning the names of the letters. The names are a way for the learner to collect information about the letters. The learner uses the letter name to create a memory file for each letter. The name "provides a means of bonding together all of one's experiences with the to-be-learned concept" (Adams, 1990). As children interact with books, the comments of parents and caregivers about letter names and features of letters are added to the file and integrated with this initial information. With time and experience, children add information about the sound correspondences for the letters. One advantage to teaching children the names of the letters is that often the name holds a clue to the sound of the letter. Children also begin to notice the probable letter combinations in which the letter might be found.

Many children have learned the alphabet before coming to school. Often this learning began before the age of 3. This means that children have had a substantial amount of time to add information to their files and to sort the information to determine what was significant. In most cases, the children have also had the benefit of an interested, knowing other to guide their explorations. Children entering the classroom today will come from very diverse backgrounds in terms of their literacy experiences. The classroom teacher will be challenged to get those children with less letter knowledge ready for reading in a very short period of time, so it is important to remember that it is the wealth and variety of literacy experiences that have led the most successful children to the knowledge about letters that they now possess. These same rich literacy experiences are appropriate for the children who have not yet had the opportunity to share these experiences (Morrow, Strickland, & Woo, 1998). Children who have not yet been given the opportunity need to manipulate magnetic letters, form letters out of clay, point out the letters of their name when they see them in books and on signs, sing songs about letters, and listen to alphabet books being read. It is important to note that although letter knowledge is a significant predictor of success in reading, teaching children with limited alphabet knowledge to identify the letters of the alphabet does not in itself ensure reading success. The knowledge children acquire about literacy and its uses as they are learning to identify the letters of the alphabet may be as significant as learning the letters themselves (Smolkin & Yaden, 1992). How children learn the alphabet and whether or not that learning is tied to other literacy and learning experiences is equally important. By immersing children in a variety of alphabet experiences, most of which involve reading and writing, children are able to make functional and lasting use of their alphabet knowledge.

Most children have learned many of the names for the letters of the alphabet prior to coming to school (Mason, 1980; McCormick & Mason, 1986). An important goal of kindergarten programs is to reinforce the alphabet learning that has already taken place and to extend that learning to unknown letters. Research indicates that children have a stronger grasp of upper-case letters than lower-case letters. The teacher will assess the extent of the children's alphabet knowledge early in the school year to ensure that children are able to recognize and discriminate all letters with ease and fluency (Mason, 1980; Snow et al., 1998).

Assessment of Alphabet Knowledge

Whatever the age of the child, the first thing a teacher will want to know is what the child already knows about the alphabet. The goal of our instruction should always be to meet children at the edge of their ability and have them do with support what they are not yet able to do independently (Vygotsky, 1962). For learning the alphabet, this may mean administering a simple alphabet assessment like the one in Figure 5-1, or it may mean anecdotally recording children's use of the alphabet in reading or writing. When assessing alphabet knowledge, the teacher will want to know all the understandings the child has about the alphabet (see p. 58). Can the child name the letter? Does he know the sound the letter represents? Does she understand that the letter has an upper case and a lower case? Does he know that the letters are in a specific order? Does she know a word that begins with a specific letter? There are many pieces of information that will inform classroom instruction, but this information should be gathered over time. If a teacher chose to use the assessment shown in Figure 5-1, initially the teacher would ask the child only to identify the letter. If the child was unable to do so, the teacher might ask if he or she knew the sound the letter made or a word that started with the letter. On another day the teacher might use this assessment to ask children

Figure 5-1. Alphabet Assessment

A	P	Z	Q	X	L	M
C	I	N	F	T	D	
S	E	R	U	B	K	
W	Y	G	O	J	H	V
a	p	z	q	x	l	m
c	i	n	f	t	d	a
s	e	r	u	b	k	g
w	y	g	o	j	h	v

about the sounds for the letters or a word that begins with the letter. It is important to assess children so that instruction meets the needs of children, but assessment should never exhaust the child, and whenever possible assessment should take place in the context of the regular classroom routine.

Very young children have a distinct advantage in learning the alphabet if parents and caregivers attend to the child's interest in the alphabet as part of the child's daily routine. It is the advantage of time and attention. After a child has

Figure 5-1. (continued)

Alphabet Assessment

	Letter	Sound	Word	Notes		Letter	Sound	Word	Notes
A					a				
P					p				
Z					z				
Q					q				
X					x				
L					l				
M					m				
C					c				
I					i				
N					n				
F					f				
T					t				
D					d				
					a				
S					s				
E					e				
R					r				
U					u				
B					b				
K					k				
					g				
W					w				
Y					y				
G					g				
O					o				
J					j				
H					h				
V					v				

learned the alphabet song and begun to develop the concept of an alphabet that contains a series of things that can be named, parents and caregivers help the child to understand the distinctive features of the letters by pointing out the letters in the child's environment. Children are given the opportunity to interact with letters on children's television shows such as *Sesame Street*, with objects in their homes such as magnetic letters, and with objects in their environment such as the *o* on the Cheerios™ box. These interactions usually take place in an informal playful setting, but they are often observed and extended by an interested adult (McGee & Richgels, 1989). The child's natural fascination is recognized and supported so that it becomes a foundational piece of learning to read.

This same interest in the alphabet can be nurtured in the classroom. The teacher assumes the role of interested adult, supports children as they are learning the alphabet, and provisions the classroom with sets of manipulative alphabet letters made of a variety of materials in a variety of colors, sizes, and fonts. Children use wood, plastic, foam, magnetic, or sandpaper alphabet sets to sort, classify, and sequence the letters. The teacher supplies children with materials such as clay, sand trays, shaving cream, and finger paint to practice letter formation. These materials help children to feel the shape of the letter. The teacher encourages children to write the letters in the air using big, distinctive strokes and to pair with other children to become the letters by using their bodies to make letter shapes. Children are also given the opportunity to write letters using pencils, crayons, and markers. An assortment of materials and a variety of experiences allows children to learn the name of the letter, the distinctive features of the letter, and how to form the letter. This multisensory approach allows all children to find an avenue to learning the alphabet and helps children to become flexible in their understanding of letter names.

The classroom environment is purposefully print-rich and arranged in ways that encourage children to interact with the alphabet in print. The teacher and children work together to create an alphabet frieze, collect environmental print to illustrate sound and word associations for each letter, and make class letter books. The library corner will contain a variety of alphabet books, picture dictionaries, and a first thesaurus or simple word books.

In any classroom, almost the whole alphabet can be learned by using the most meaningful information in a child's world: one's name and the names of one's classmates. These are very powerful letters. Initially, many children believe that a letter is a direct representation of a person; for example, *M* is Michelle (Dyson, 1984). With time and experience, they begin to recognize their name in its entirety and realize that many words that are not their name also contain the same letter. They begin to understand that the letters represent sounds. The teacher capitalizes on the interest children have in the letters of their name by focusing children's attention on these letters as often as possible. Children's names should be displayed in the classroom in any appropriate location: on cubbies, tabletop workspaces, coat hangers, job charts, sign-in books, library cards, lunch count charts, and countless other places. Perhaps most important, post children's names with the alphabet chart. An instant photo with the child's name written on it is an ideal name tag for young children. Children's attention can also be drawn to the letters of their names at transition times. The teacher will ask all of the children whose name begins with a specific letter to line up, or ask everyone whose name starts with the same letter as a specific word, such as *fish,* to line up.

In addition to these experiences, the teacher helps children to name, identify, and develop sound associations for the letters of the alphabet as they read and write during literacy activities throughout the day. During shared reading, the teacher focuses on specific letters in the story. After the teacher and the children have read through the story, the class returns to the text and the teacher asks children to point to a specific letter, circle the letter with a Wikki Stix™ (a wax-covered string that sticks to the page without adhering permanently), or cover the letter with highlighter tape. After the children have identified the letter and often its corresponding sound, the teacher rereads the story so that children can connect what they have learned to the text they have been reading. The teacher might also follow up the reading by giving all of the children Wikki Stix™ or Post-it™ flags and going on a letter hunt. The children will then search the classroom environment and mark the letter they are learning.

Children are also asked to identify letters as the class works on shared writing activities. The teacher and children work together to write a text about a shared experience. As they write, the teacher asks children to name letters that are needed for writing some of the words. The teacher carefully chooses the letters that he or she asks the children to name and bases the questions on an ongoing assessment of the children's alphabet knowledge. Children will be asked to identify the letters that are partially known to build letter recognition and assure letter knowledge is secure. For example, the teacher might have noticed that Thomas identifies the letter *T* at the beginning his name, but is unsure if he could pick it out on the alphabet chart. To assess Thomas's knowledge, the teacher will ask him to show him or her the letter as the class writes their daily message. Some children will be asked to identify the target letter from a limited set of letter choices. Thomas might be asked to look at the section of the alphabet chart that contains the letters *S, s, T, t, U, u* to locate the letter *T*. When young children have limited alphabet knowledge, making the appropriate choice from twenty-six upper- and lower-case letters is too complex a task. As children increase the number of known letters and become more proficient at letter identification, the teacher will offer less support to the learner. After the class has finished writing the message, the teacher and children will reread the message, and as they do so they may look for a specific letter, circling it when it appears in the message. Another way to help children learn the alphabet during shared writing experiences is to give each child an individual whiteboard and dry erase marker. The teacher writes, asking for the children's help in identifying a needed letter. When the children have identified the letter, they will be asked to make the letter on their board as the teacher writes it on the chalkboard. A quick visual check of the children will tell the teacher which children can identify and write the letter correctly.

Another way that the teacher enables children to learn the alphabet is by helping them think about the distinctive features of each letter. During transition times the teacher can play a game of "Which Letter Am I?" in which the teacher gives the children a simple riddle that will lead them to guess the letter name. As the children listen to the clues, they think about the shape of the letter, its position relative to other letters, and a sound or word association. For example, the teacher might say: "I am completely round. I come after the letter *n*. I am at the beginning of the word *octopus*. Which letter am I?"

An important component of learning the alphabet is independent writing. As children write, they often name the letter they are writing. They focus on the distinctive features of the letter as they labor over its construction. This vocalization, combined with the physical movement involved in forming the letter, is very powerful in helping children to learn the letter. Children often make several tries at a letter before they determine that the letter is just right. The repetition of making the letters over and over as they work on independent writing solidifies the identification of the letter. In the attempts children make to get the letter just right, often with many erasures, they are constructing a definition of each letter. They are determining what makes a *B* a *B* or an *m* an *m*. In the process of construction, children work with the letter many times until recognition is automatic, making letter recognition fast and fluent. The teacher can support children in this process by talking about the letter, what the letter looks like, and how to make the letter. The process of discussing the features and formation of the letter may prevent the erasing that interferes with children writing with fluency. The teacher may use rhymes and poems to help children remember the strokes for correct formation of the letters. For example, when making an *a* (lowercase), the teacher might say to the children, "The little alligator swims all the way around, then goes to the side of the circle and climbs straight down." After children have practiced making the letter, they repeat the name of the letter they have written.

Young children need opportunities to play with the alphabet. Center activities can provide these opportunities. An alphabet center can be provisioned with a variety of tactile, manipulative alphabet sets and letter tiles. Children can trace, sort, match, and order these letter sets. It is suggested that one of these letter sets be magnetic letters. The center might contain board games such as alphabet bingo and alphabet blocks and puzzles. The center should also contain tools for making the letters of the alphabet. Materials such as play dough or clay, a sand tray, and a Magna Doodle™ provide varied and interesting practice with letter formation. Alphabet stamps and ink pads can be used to create messages as children are learning the letters. The center should contain alphabet strips or charts so children can check their work against a model.

In addition to teaching children the names of the letters, the teacher will also support children as they learn the sound associations for the letters. The first associations children make with letter sounds are related to their names. Just as children make the most meaningful associations for letter naming with the letters of their names, so also are these the most meaningful letters for making sound associations. From the very first shared reading and shared writing experiences, the teacher will gently begin to draw children's attention to the sound associations for each letter and letter combination. As children become more attentive to the print, the teacher will capitalize on the opportunity to make explicit connections between sounds and letters. For more detailed information on teaching letter-sound associations see chapter 6.

Knowledge of the alphabet is important to reading success. This makes teaching the alphabet important, but this statement must come with a caution. It is not necessary to teach children the alphabet before they are allowed to try out being a reader or a writer. These are roles children take on with joy and confidence as young children and they should be encouraged to do so. It is not enough to teach children only the alphabet. Knowing the alphabet is more than fluent naming, and only a small part of the skills, strategies, and psychological processes needed to become a fluent reader. Children need to understand that the alphabet is a part of their journey toward reading and writing, and the letters and their associated sounds are one tool they will use to read new and unseen words. Learning the alphabet should be *a part* of learning to read, not *apart* from learning to read, and not a prerequisite to reading.

When Children Are Having Difficulty Learning the Alphabet

Learning the letters of the alphabet is a much easier task for some children than for others. Many children have had rich preschool experiences in which the teacher has read stories to them, written notes to them, and displayed meaningful print in their environment. Many children have had the opportunity to play with the letters of the alphabet. They have formed the letters with clay, placed the letters in jigsaw puzzles, and painted the letters with finger paint. These children find it a relatively simple task to learn the alphabet. Other children have had relatively little experience with the alphabet. Initially, their instruction should include rich experiences that require them to interact with the alphabet. All children should have the opportunity to learn the alphabet by making connections with the letters in reading, in writing, and through multisensory experiences.

Sometimes, despite a wealth of experiences and competent classroom instruction, children have difficulty learning the letters of the alphabet. When this happens the teacher needs to take the extra time to help children learn the letters of the alphabet. Although it is possible to begin reading words and to read very simple patterned books without knowing all of the letters of the alphabet, to transition to independent reading a child must learn to make fast, fluent recognition of the letters of the alphabet. Letter recognition must become effortless regardless of the size of the print or the type of font in which the letter is printed.

To help these children learn the alphabet, begin with what the child knows best. Most often these are the letters of the child's name. Talk about the letters, the shape of the letter, the pattern for correctly producing the letter, and the name of the letter. Some children find it easy to identify the sound of the letter but have difficulty remembering the name. When this happens allow the child to label the letter by the sound and help the child to learn the name. Be specific with the child. When the child looks at the letter *b* and says that's /b/, tell the child that that is correct—it does make the sound /b/ and the name of the letter is *b*. When children are having difficulty learning the alphabet, it is important to be direct, specific, and to connect what they are learning to what they already know. As the child is learning the sound and the name of the letter, it may be helpful for them to learn a word that begins with the letter. For children who have difficulty learning the alphabet, the word association for the letter should initially remain consistent across contexts. Establishing a single word association for the letter simplifies the learning connection until the child is fluent with the letter identification. This means that the word association on the alphabet chart, the desk alphabet strip, and the child's alphabet book should all be the same. The consistency of the name, sound, and word association will support the child until letter recognition is automatic.

When the letter is introduced to the child, model the correct formation of the letter. Make the letter large enough for the child to easily see the motor pattern used. Verbalize the directions for making the letter. For example, when making the letter *h,* the teacher will model, saying, "Down, up, and a hump—*h.*" It is important that the child repeat the name of the letter each time the letter is practiced. Have the child copy the letter, repeating the directions. To reinforce learning the letter, ask the child to make the letter in the air, trace the letter on a desktop, write the letter with a wet paintbrush on a chalkboard, or draw the letter in a salt or sand tray. This repetition creates a motor pattern that is associated with the name of the letter.

As children become confident with the letters of their name, move on to other easy-to-identify letters. These may be letters from meaningful words such as *mom* and *stop,* or they may be letters that the teacher judges to be especially useful to the child because of books the class is reading or letters in high-frequency words the child is using in writing. The teacher will want to avoid introducing letters that might be easily confused at the same time, for example *b* and *d.* Teach the child one of the letters, and when it is overlearned introduce the second letter.

To help children become fast and fluent in letter recognition, the teacher asks children to sort letters, putting all the letters that are the same together. Magnetic letters are especially useful for this purpose. Children should do this quickly and name each letter as it is sorted into the correct group. Letters can also be sorted by case—children might be asked to put all of the uppercase *W*s together and the lowercase *w*'s together—or sorted by shape—all of the letters with circles go together, all of the letters with sticks go together. When sorting letters, the teacher will want to start the sorting process by looking at common features such as letters with circles, letters with sticks, letters with humps. The sorts might move on to sort between two letters. Children would be asked to put all of the *r*'s in one group and all of the *l*'s in another. The sorts become more complex as the child is more familiar with the alphabet. It is also important to remember to build on what the child knows, so early sorts will include one letter the child knows, perhaps a letter from his or her name, and a letter the child is learning. The child will repeat the name of the letter as it is being sorted into a group. The sorts should avoid close confusers, such as *p* and *q,* until children have had a significant amount of experience looking at letters and have built a large number of known letters. The teacher might also ask children to put the letters in order or to match letters to a printed alphabet. Sorting helps children to develop automatic identification of the letter while building the ability to recognize the letter in a variety of contexts.

It is important to emphasize that this very focused type of instruction is needed for only a small number of the children who are learning the alphabet and that this type of instruction should occupy only a small portion of the instructional day. It is also important to note that children do not need to learn all of the letters of the alphabet before they begin reading or writing. Letter identification is not prerequisite to reading and writing, it is developed as children are reading and writing.

Using Alphabet Books

The alphabet book is an essential tool for teaching and learning the alphabet. This is especially true for children who are having difficulty learning the letters of the alphabet. Having a consistent resource that can be read and reread supports children's emerging understanding of the alphabet. Earlier in this chapter, we listed understandings that children need to develop about the alphabet. Many of these understandings can be developed as children listen to alphabet books being read. Children learn to identify the names, cases, distinctive features, order, sound associations, and probable combinations of the letters. Alphabet books give children the opportunity to identify objects and explore concepts, supporting emergent and beginning readers in their oral language development and promoting letter and sound identification (Chaney, 1993). Alphabet books create environments where children can analyze the features of the letters and explore the orientation of the letter to the page.

In a study of children's experiences with alphabet books, Smolkin and Yaden (1992) found that children were not only learning the expected letter and sound associations, they were also developing a variety of understandings about how book learning is accomplished in school. Children learned that books were places they could make identifications, test knowledge, and make connections between their world and the world of books. They learned that they could play with the sounds of language and discover word meanings, and they learned that books were places where they could wonder and speculate. When children have the opportunity to hear alphabet books being read over and over, they develop concepts of print, understanding of metalinguistic terms, ways of knowing, and letter knowledge.

While alphabet books are invaluable in helping children to learn the alphabet, not all alphabet books are equally appropriate for this task. The best book for teaching children the alphabet depends on what children already know about the alphabet. Children with very little alphabet knowledge will benefit most from having a very simple alphabet book to read and reread each day. Ideally the book will have one letter, both uppercase and lowercase, on each page, as well as a clear illustration of one object that begins with the letter and the name of the object on the page. Suse MacDonald's (1992) *Alphabetics* is an excellent alphabet book for emergent readers. Children with very little alphabet knowledge also need to listen to a variety of alphabet books being read aloud. These alphabet books should be more complex and give children the opportunity to puzzle out the distinctive features of the letter, develop sound association for the letter, and expand their vocabularies.

As children learn more about the alphabet, they benefit from having a more complex alphabet book to read. Alphabet books such as Robert Bender's (1996) *A to Z Beastly Jamboree* or *The Letters Are Lost* by Lisa Campbell Ernst (1996) have a single line of text and very supportive illustrations. These books move beyond letter identification to letter-sound associations. The teacher supports students at this level by reading aloud more complex books, often books that use alliteration as a major feature to help children learn letter-sound associations. Alphabet books help children to become proficient with letter identification and sound associations and can be used to help children expand vocabulary and develop concepts.

Every emergent and beginning reader should have an alphabet book in his or her independent reading basket. When choosing an alphabet book for a child to read and reread to learn letter identification and letter-sound associations, the teacher will want to consider the child's level of alphabet knowledge, understanding of concepts of print, and general reading level. The teacher will also consider the characteristics of the alphabet book. Features the teacher might consider when choosing an alphabet book include the complexity of the text; the quality of the illustrations; the conceptual difficulty of the text; the literary attributes of the book, such as an emphasis on rhyme or alliteration; and the genre of the text, story, object identification, or concept development. By carefully matching the capabilities of the child and the characteristics of the alphabet book, the teacher chooses an alphabet book for each child that challenges their thinking and develops the needed understandings about the alphabet.

The final consideration in choosing an alphabet book for a child is the teacher's or student's motivation for doing so. Alphabet books come not only in a variety of shapes and sizes but also in a variety of types. There are alphabet books that help children with letter naming, alphabet books that promote understanding of alliteration, alphabet books that promote letter-sound associations through picture hunts, alphabet books that promote letter identification by examining the visual details of the letters, puzzle alphabet books, concept alphabet books, and alphabet books that are good read-aloud stories.

Simple Alphabet Books That Promote Naming the Letters

When most people think of alphabet books, they imagine the type of alphabet book that helps children to learn to name the letters of the alphabet. The format is simple, clear, and consistent. Each page contains a letter, an illustration of an object that begins with that letter, and the printed word for that object. David

McPhail's (1989) *Animals A to Z* is an example of this type of text. The page for the letter *V* depicts a vulture playing a violin. The vulture is standing on a branch with a vase of violets. The text reads "Vulture." The letter *V* is printed clearly on the page. These books are easy for the youngest readers to tackle if they are familiar with the object used as an association for the letter. In one beautifully illustrated alphabet book, the author, who is British, has used marmalade as the association for the letter *M*. Marmalade is very common to the child in England but much less so to the child in the United States. Lack of familiarity with the object makes this an inappropriate book for initially learning the alphabet for some children. It is important to ensure that children are familiar with the objects being named, especially when working with children learning English as a second language.

Alphabet Books That Promote Letter-Sound Associations Through Alliteration

These alphabet books help children to develop sound associations for the letters. The text is alliterative and playful. They are the kind of sentences and phrases that feel good in your mouth and sound good to your ear. *Alphabet Soup: A Feast of Letters* by Scott Gustafson (1994) is an alliterative alphabet book. This is a fanciful story of an otter who holds a potluck housewarming. The guests come with food that they like: "Bear was the very best baker who baked the most beautiful breads…braided breads and brown bran muffins, buttermilk biscuits and buttery buns…all these were bundled into big baskets and brought to the banquet by Bear." Children delight in the rhythm and resonance of the text and make connections between the alliterative phrases and the sound of the letters. These books are excellent for helping children to make connections between sounds and letters; however, the text is too complex for emergent and beginning readers. They are great for reading aloud to children and the illustrations are often rich in detail, which invites children to pour over the pictures again and again.

Alphabet Books That Promote Letter-Sound Associations Through Picture Hunts

From Letter to Letter by Teri Sloat (1989) is a superb example of an alphabet book that helps children to learn letters and letter-sound associations. These associations are developed as children search the illustrations for objects that begin with each letter. In Sloat's book the page for the letter *d* shows a large uppercase *D* filled with captivating drawings of dinosaurs, dolls, drums, dice, deer, daffodils, dolphins, as well as dogs that spill out onto the rest of the page and climb onto a large lowercase *d* that sits among a patch of dandelions. The illustrations lead the children across the page as they identify each object. Naming the objects gives a child the opportunity to hear the sound of the letter at the beginning of the word repeated over and over again. The book invites discussion. Children will want to know what an *echidna* is and who lives in a Quonset hut. This discussion leads to expanded vocabularies, an important foundation for reading success.

Alphabet Books That Promote Letter Identification Through Examination of Visual Details

One of the keys to fluent alphabet identification is understanding which features are significant to the letter. These alphabet books show the letters being formed. In *Albert's Alphabet* by Leslie Tryon (1991), Albert, the school handyman, is asked to construct an alphabet for the school playground. He uses a variety of materials to cut, hammer, mortar, and screw together every letter of the alphabet. As children carefully examine each illustration, they develop an understanding of the features that are significant to the letter.

Alphabet Books to Read Aloud

All alphabet books are environments for letter identification and discussion, but some alphabet books have a story line that makes it especially appropriate as a read-aloud. Other read-aloud choices contain a strong sense of rhythm and rhyme. A class favorite is *The Monster Book of ABC Sounds* by Alan Snow (1991). In this book Snow tells the story of a rat and a monster playing a game of hide-and-seek. Each facing page forms a rhyme. The letters *b* and *c* read, "A monster pops out from behind the door. BOO! While three cunning rats sneak a look 'neath the floor. Cooee!" Children delight in watching the rats and monster chase each other, and what could be better than chiming in to make each and every sound? Alphabet books make great read-alouds when there is a sense of playfulness to the text, when they invite discussion, and when they create that "read it again" feeling.

Alphabet Puzzle Books

When one considers criteria for a good alphabet book, at the top of the list is having a letter on each page with a clear and evident picture association for the letter. Alphabet puzzle books break this rule. In these books, the point is to puzzle out the letter of the alphabet being alluded to by using information in the text and knowledge of the alphabet to decide on an answer. George Shannon's (1996) *Tomorrow's Alphabet* is a puzzle book. Shannon has used a twist to the classic "A is for apple" format to create an alphabet book that is thought-provoking for young children. For the letter *k* the text reads, "K is for tomato—tomorrow's KETCHUP." The format asks children to use their alphabet knowledge and to think ahead to solve the puzzle of why *K* is for *tomato*. Puzzle books delight children who are somewhat familiar with the alphabet but can be difficult for emergent readers. Even when you are reading this book aloud to young children, it is important to discuss the book and explore the puzzles and how to solve them together. These books beg the teacher to ask the question "How did you know?"

Alphabet Concept Books

Perhaps the most common type of alphabet book is the concept book, in which the author's intent is to explore a topic. The alphabet is an organizational tool for sharing the information about the topic. A primary example of such a book is *Amazon Alphabet* by Martin and Tanis Jordan. This beautifully illustrated book shares information about the animals of the Amazon region. "A, a is for Agouti eating Brazil nuts." Concept books such as this are interesting, complex, and fact-filled. Because of their difficult text and concepts, these books are most usually more appropriate for reading aloud to children and are used as a resource for primary-age researchers. They are seldom appropriate for independent reading.

Sets of Alphabet Books

In recent years a new type of alphabet book has been developed that differs from its predecessors in size and scope. These are little alphabet books, perfect for small hands. Most contain 8–12 pages of text. Each book contains information about only one letter. The books are sold as a set that contains all 26 letters. The books show both the uppercase and lowercase form of the letter. In some books the letters appear on each page, in others they appear only on the first page. The following 6–10 pages show a single object that begins with the target letter and the word for that object. Each set of books has interesting features unique to that set. One set of books has a velvety letter on the cover to give children the opportunity to experience the letter tactilely by tracing it with a finger. Some of the sets are developed around children's names, a powerful connection to letter identification. One of the sets prompts children to think about the order of the alphabet by introducing the next letter of the alphabet on the last page of the book. One of the sets uses many of the words from objects pictured in the book to make a sentence. Each set is unique and makes a wonderful addition to any preschool or kindergarten classroom. They provide an opportunity for letter identification, vocabulary development, and the development of emergent reading behaviors.

On a recent visit to a kindergarten classroom, a small group of boys organized a guessing game around a set of these books. One of the boys chose a book and asked the other boys to guess the name of the object he was looking at. He gave them clues and showed them the cover of the book, which displays the letter of the alphabet. The boys stayed engaged in their game for an extended period of time. It was meeting the needs of every child in the group. The most knowledgeable child was pushing himself to think of clues without giving away the answer. Two of the boys were attending closely and trying to compete to see who would give the correct answer first, and one child was guessing randomly. The other boys would redirect his random guesses to the correct letter of the alphabet. The conversation was rich and filled with higher level thinking and problem solving. This is the type of play with the alphabet that children generate when there are time, materials, high expectations, and opportunities for engagement in the classroom.

CHAPTER 6

Teaching Phonics

A Definition of Phonics

In previous chapters we have defined and described the components of phonics instruction. In this chapter we define phonics and describe how phonics instruction works in a literature-based classroom. Although the term *phonics* evokes highly politicized and confusing responses from various experts, the definition is quite simple. Phonics is the relationship between the oral sounds and the letters of a written language. As stated in chapter 1, phonics is one source of information, or cues, available to readers. An understanding of phonics and how to apply that knowledge is critical to the ability to read accurately. However, as we have noted, a reader using only phonics cues will not read with comprehension. Phonics must be taught in conjunction with the other cues of meaning and language structure for a reader to read with understanding and fluency. "The ultimate goal of phonics instruction is for children to use this knowledge when reading and writing" (Fege, Fowler, & Anzalone, 1998).

The teacher helps children to understand phonics generalizations about the following:

Consonants

Children generally develop an understanding of initial consonants first and an understanding of final and medial sounds later. Understanding initial consonants is important to beginning reading. Children also base their beginning learning about consonant sounds on the letter-sound relationships found in their names. The letter names of some consonants (*b, d, f, j, k, m, n, p, q, r, s, t, v, z*) are similar to the sounds they represent, and for some children these are easier to learn. It is not uncommon for children to hear the predominant consonant in a word. Evidence of this is often found in children's beginning writing. Teachers help children build on this knowledge of consonant sounds to say words slowly and listen for the other sounds.

Consonant diagraphs. These are two letters that represent one speech sound; for example, *ch, wh, sh,* and *th.*

Blends. These are sounds that go together when making words; for example, *gr, bl, and st.* The sound for each letter can be heard when the word is stretched out or spoken slowly, but the sounds of the two letters work together.

Rimes

A rime is the part of a one-syllable word or a syllable that begins with a vowel. The beginning part of the word or syllable is the onset. For example, in the word *sick,* the *s* is the onset and *-ick* is the rime. Rimes are not the same as rhymes. However, there is a relationship. The words *hat, bat,* and *cat* all have the same rime, and in addition they rhyme. Learning rimes, or word patterns, increases the number of words children can read and write. Understanding how rimes work can help children problem solve new words. It is important to note that nearly 500 words can be derived from the following set of 37 rimes (Adams, 1990):

-ack	*-all*	*-ain*	*-ake*	*-ale*	*-ame*	*-an*	*-ank*	*-ap*	*-ash*
-at	*-ate*	*-aw*	*-ay*	*-eat*	*-ell*	*-est*	*-ice*	*-ick*	*-ide*
-ight	*-ill*	*-in*	*-ine*	*-ing*	*-ink*	*-ip*	*-ir*	*-ock*	*-oke*
-op	*-ore*	*-or*	*-uck*	*-ug*	*-ump*	*-unk*			

Vowels

Short vowels. In a literature-based classroom, children encounter vowels when they are reading, but short vowels are formally introduced after children have an understanding of initial and final consonants and begin to use word patterns. Short vowels are the sounds of the letter *a, e, i, o,* and *u* heard in words such as *fat, pet, sit, pot,* and *fun.*

Long vowels. Long vowels are taught by helping children to make generalizations about long vowel patterns, such as the final *e* pattern; two-vowel patterns such as *ay, ee, oa;* and a vowel at the end of single syllable words, such as *so, she, me.* The degree of usefulness for teaching and learning these patterns varies.

Vowel variants. These letter-sound relationships are often inconsistent and difficult to learn in isolation. Teaching these sounds as rimes makes them more useful to children. Examples are *oi, oy, aw,* and *r*-controlled vowels.

Structural Analysis

Children learn about prefixes, suffixes, and inflectional endings, such as *-s, -ed,* and *-ing* (Fege et al., 1998).

It is important to state that phonics instruction is most effective when surrounded by oral language and good literature. Children must be able to discriminate the sounds and identify the letters in words and apply that knowledge to determining unknown words, while remembering that the goal of reading is to understand the words.

Phonics Instruction in Curriculum-Based and Student-Centered Classrooms

At this point, we feel it is important to discuss the differences in phonics instruction in curriculum-based and student-centered classrooms. In a curriculum-based classroom, the sequence of phonics instruction is determined by the curriculum. The teacher instructs using this prescribed sequence, regardless of the needs of the children. These curricula can be purchased through basal publishers, or they can be written by a school district or mandated by a state. Many trade book publishers now publish a scope and sequence curriculum in response to the political climate of the times. Although these curricula may not be as prescriptive as others, they do offer the teacher a sequence of instruction. It should not be construed that we are opposed to a curriculum. School districts must have a program of study that outlines what students will learn. However, it is how the curriculum is used that defines the instruction.

Let's examine phonics instruction in a curriculum-based classroom. In one classroom, the teacher introduces sounds and letters in isolation in a prescribed sequence as determined by the authors of the curriculum. The teacher's manual guides the teacher in deciding the instruction for the class. For example, if the program dictates that the letter *m* be taught in lesson 12, then all children in the class are taught the letter *m*. The teacher shows the children an *m*, says the sound *m*, and asks the children to repeat the sound while looking at the letter. The teacher might read a story containing many *m* words and then ask the students to practice writing the letter *m*, both upper- and lowercase. A picture of a monkey or other easily recognized animal or object whose name begins with *m* might be attached to the worksheet for practicing letters. In this classroom, Mary, Maria, and Michael learn about the letter *m*. These children probably recognize and write the letter *m*. They do not need to spend time learning what they already know, but the curriculum is driving the instruction, not the needs of the students.

Not all curricula is quite so rigid. Many incorporate quality literature for children right from the beginning. These programs are based on the theory that children should learn to read by experiencing literature through hearing it read aloud and through reading it themselves. Sounds and letters are introduced within the context of meaningful text. Many of the publishers provide very short, little trade books designed to be used for teaching certain letters and sounds. These little books also offer support to the reader. In the books for emerging readers, the pictures illustrate the text very clearly. Print is placed in the same location on a page. The text is highly predictable, following a repetitive pattern. All of these characteristics assist the reader with a successful reading experience. Teacher materials in these programs provide information to the teacher on modeling lessons on strategies, vocabulary, and skills. Also included are the black line masters for students to practice skills. While these curricula support a teacher in reading instruction, the curriculum as outlined in the materials drives the instruction.

Now let's look at a student-centered classroom. In this classroom, the teacher makes instructional decisions according to the needs of the children. The goal in this class is for the children to develop problem-solving strategies so they can unlock, or decode, the meaning of text and read independently at the appropriate level. The teacher in this classroom determines what the students' strengths and needs are and plans instruction accordingly.

Students are grouped and regrouped flexibly to receive needed instruction. A teacher may find that some of the students still need work in ending sounds. The teacher brings these children together as a group to work on hearing and reading the ending sounds of words. This group may be chanting familiar rhymes, using magnetic letters to make words with the same ending sounds, or stretching out words prior to writing them. This same teacher may find that several students are able to independently and accurately read text written at an emergent level. Examples of emergent books are *Have You Seen My Duckling?* by Nancy Tafuri (1984) or *Do You Want to Be My Friend?* by Eric Carle (1971). These students are grouped so the teacher can provide instruction in reading strategies and skills that will move these students to reading at a more challenging level. A third group of students may need to review consonant diagraphs. The teacher works with this group to add words to a class chart of consonant diagraphs. The group might also read a book with many examples of consonant diagraphs, such as *Sheep on a Ship* by Nancy Shaw (1989). To practice fluency and automaticity, a pair of children "read the room," using a special star-tipped pointer to point to words that have been written on charts, on the chalkboard, or on the wall. In the student-centered classroom, the teacher determines what needs to be taught, when it needs to be taught or practiced, and who needs to be taught or to practice a particular skill or strategy. Some lessons are for the whole class, some are for small groups, and some are for individual students. The teacher makes these decisions based on knowing the students by continually assessing them.

Assessment

Assessment begins with determining what a child knows and can do. "The primary goal of assessment is to gather data to inform teaching. If assessment does not result in improved instruction, then its value in school diminishes greatly" (Fountas & Pinnell, 1996). Assessment of children's phonics knowledge guides the teacher in appropriately planning and matching phonics instruction for each student. It is important to assess students early in the school year and to continually assess progress throughout the year. Assessment takes place in the context of reading and writing activities. The teacher assesses the students' use of the following when reading and writing:

- consonants (initial, final, and medial)
- rimes
- diagraphs
- blends
- vowels
- structural analysis of words (Fege, et al., 1998)

In a literature-based, student-centered classroom, the teacher will also want to know what students know about print, how well they comprehend what they read or is read to them, and if they enjoy and attend to reading and writing. All of this can be determined through a number of assessment activities.

"Marie Clay's *An Observation Survey of Early Literacy Achievement* (1993a) provides the most practical procedures and richest source of information currently available" (Fountas & Pinnell, 1996). Some of the procedures developed by Clay can easily be adapted to fit the needs and styles in a particular school or classroom. Other sources for assessment are student retellings, anecdotal records, and checklists. We will first describe procedures developed by Clay, then explain the other sources for assessment.

Letter Identification

During the letter identification or alphabet assessment task, the child is provided with a sheet of paper containing the letters of the alphabet in both upper- and lowercase and a typeset *a* and *g*. The child is asked to identify the letters by name, by sound, or by furnishing a word that begins with that letter. This assessment provides the teacher with important information that will help to direct instructional planning. Research has found that prereaders' letter knowledge was found to be the single best predictor of first-year reading achievement (Adams, 1990). However, children who can identify the letter names can attend to visual details of print but may not realize that letter symbols represents sounds. It is important for the teacher to follow up on the child's ability to name letters with asking the child to identify the sounds. The child who provides a word for a letter, such as *Mommy* for *m*, may misunderstand the letter for the meaning of a word and may not understand the letter as a symbol.

Figure 6-1 shows the results of a completed letter identification assessment for Stephanie. This student is in first grade and in November exhibits confusion between *u* and *v* and between *b* and *d*. The teacher, Mrs. Kurtz, comments that the student read the letters quickly, which would indicate that the child feels comfortable with the alphabet. The teacher knows she can build on the child's knowledge of letters during reading instruction.

Figure 6-1. Letter Identification Score Sheet

Name _Stephanie____   Date *11/30*

	letter	sound	word		letter	sound	word
A	✓			a	✓		
F	✓			f	✓		
K	✓			k	✓		
P	✓			p	✓		
W	✓			w	✓		
Z	✓			z	X /sc		
B	✓			b	d		
H	✓			h	✓		
O	✓			o	✓		
J	✓			j	✓		
U	✓			u	✓		
				a	✓		
C	✓			c	✓		
Y	✓			y	✓		
L	✓			l	✓		
Q	✓			q	P		
M	✓			m	✓		
D	✓			d	✓		
N	✓			n	✓		
S	✓			s	✓		
X	✓			x	✓		
I	✓			i	✓		
E	✓			e	✓		
G	✓			g	✓		
R	✓			r	✓		
V	u			v	u		
T	✓			t	✓		
				g	✓		

Adapted from *An Observation Survey* by Marie Clay

Word Test

The teacher asks the child to read a list of words in isolation. The teacher can use a list of high-frequency words from a published list or develop a list of words that are frequently found in the texts used in that classroom. Observing how the child problem solves any difficult words will increase the teacher's understanding of the child's capabilities. If the child reads *go* in place of *going* and *child* for *children*, the teacher knows that this child needs instruction on endings of words. Another child might read *Mom* for *Mother* and *Dad* for *Father*. This child is working on making meaning but needs work in attending to the visual information in the print.

Figure 6-2 shows Stephanie's performance on a word test. Mrs. Kurtz uses this list because it contains many high-frequency words and word patterns that the first-grade child will encounter in her reading. There are many word lists that teachers can choose to use. Stephanie knows seven words. When attempting words, Stephanie tends to rely on the initial consonant, with the notable exception of her attempts for *where, am,* and *did.* She did recognize her error with *am* but was unable to self-correct. Her response of *baby* for *did* supports the earlier assessment of the *b* and *d* confusion.

Figure 6-2. Word Test

Name: Stephanie **Date:** 11/30

Word Test 6 correct

can ✓
and ✓
the ✓
pretty playground
has hat/ hat/Try it again! /no
down N/A
where come
after N/A
let N/A
here hat/hard
am me/"no"
there the-ar
over ouch
little ✓
did baby
what went
them the
one ou
like ✓
could N/A
yes ✓

NA = no attempt

Writing Vocabulary

This assessment procedure can be done with individual children or small groups of no more than five children. The children are asked to write as many words as they know, beginning with their names, in a 10-minute period. The teacher may prompt the children with some words if they appeared stumped. The teacher then asks each child to read the words on the list. The words the children can write and read demonstrate what they know about sound-letter relationships in words. This is knowledge that the child can use when reading and writing other words. The teacher can build instruction based on that knowledge.

Stephanie's writing vocabulary is demonstrated in Figure 6-3. She is able to independently write and read 24 words. Mrs. Kurtz will plan to build on Stephanie's knowledge of the rimes *ig* and *ar*. Because Stephanie knows the words *play* and *cat*, Mrs. Kurtz can also plan to help Stephanie expand her use of the rimes *ay* and *at*. Stephanie uses the inflectional ending *-ed* on *look*. Mrs. Kurtz plans to check if Stephanie uses this with other verbs or not.

Figure 6-3. Writing Vocabulary

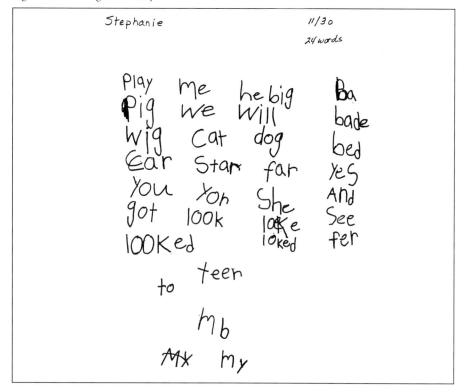

Dictation, or Hearing and Recording Sounds in Words

This assessment procedure can be done with individual children or a small group of no more than five children. The teacher reads a short message containing two sentences and asks the children to write as much of it as they can. The message is read and reread slowly so that the children have an opportunity to determine and write the letters they hear. This assessment gives the teacher valuable information about the children's phonemic awareness, ability to move from sounds to letters, and their ability to segment sounds in words.

Stephanie's work on the dictation assessment is shown in Figure 6-4. The sentences Mrs. Kurtz read to her were "The bus is coming. It will stop here to let me get on." Stephanie's writing on this task confirms her knowledge of the word *me*. She also wrote *the, is, it, stop, here,* and *to* correctly. She is able to hear and write the beginning and ending sounds to most of the words in the dictation. Medial vowel sounds are missing in several of the words, and the word beginning with a vowel was difficult for her. She wrote the inflectional *-ing.*

Using this assessment adds to Mrs. Kurtz's knowledge of Stephanie's understanding of sounds, letters, and words. Mrs. Kurtz will plan instruction that will help Stephanie to build on her knowledge of the words *it* and *stop*, showing her how to change the onsets to make new words. Mrs. Kurtz will also choose books and plan lessons to call Stephanie's attention to medial vowels. Mrs. Kurtz will ask Stephanie to work with magnetic letters, and she will write words on a whiteboard, chalkboard, and paper to help her build fluency and increase her number of known words. These activities will increase both Stephanie's reading and writing fluency.

Figure 6-4. Dictation

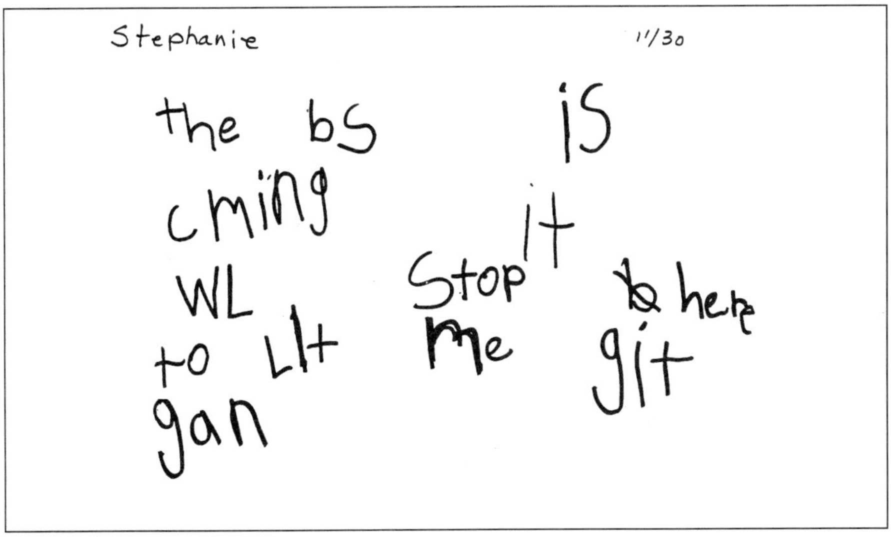

Running Record

A running record is an assessment procedure that provides a record of a childs actual reading. A teacher needs to receive training in how to take a running record.

When taking a running record, a teacher uses checks to record the child's correct reading of text, and records the incorrectly read words by writing those words over the correct words. The teacher also notes when the child corrects reading errors, and other pertinent information to understand the child's reading ability. A running record provides the teacher with information about what cues the child uses. A teacher can also learn about the phonics information a child applies or doesn't use. Running records provide valuable information for instruction matched to a child's strengths and needs.

In Figure 6-5, Mrs. Kurtz has recorded that Stephanie comments that the first sentence didn't make sense to her before she self-corrected her initial guess. A self-correction is indicated by *SC*. Stephanie also self-corrected the ending on the word *look,* again demonstrating that she understands ending sounds and the *-ed* inflectional ending. Stephanie is also attending to the visual cues in the print by looking at beginning and ending letters and sounds. She uses that information to

Figure 6-5. Running Record

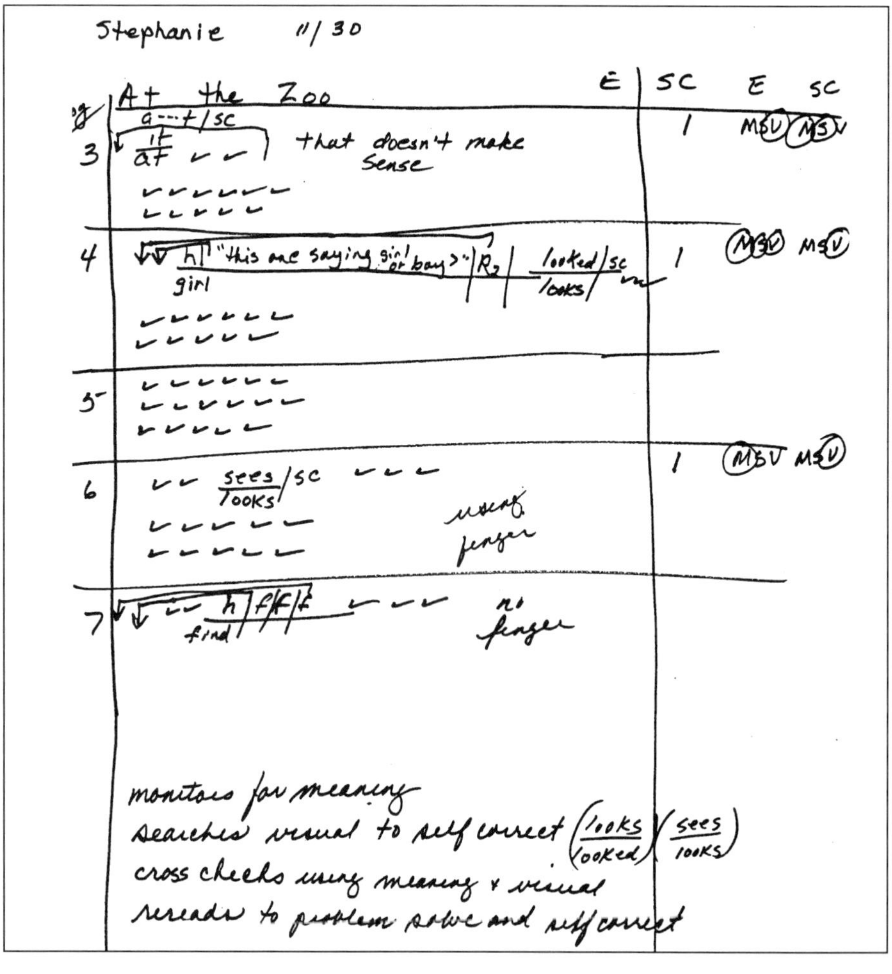

decode the words. Mrs. Kurtz notes that Stephanie is monitoring to make sure that her reading makes sense and using the visual information to check her reading. Mrs. Kurtz also records when Stephanie uses her finger to point to words. Stephanie uses this support when she is working at a place that seems difficult for her. Stephanie knows to reread to help solve problems when she is reading. Rereading is indicated by the arrows.

Because Stephanie read this book with accuracy, Mrs. Kurtz chooses books that are slightly more difficult so Stephanie can expand her skills. The next book has a few new vocabulary words but contains many of the words Stephanie knows. Mrs. Kurtz finds a book that uses words Stephanie can decode by using the words she already knows. For example, Stephanie knows the word *look*, so Mrs. Kurtz chooses a book with the verb *took* and the noun *book* in it. Mrs. Kurtz continues to make book choices that move Stephanie to increasingly difficult text.

Writing Sample

Examining a sample of a student's writing provides valuable information about that student's knowledge and application of phonics. The teacher can determine a student's knowledge of beginning, ending, and medial consonants; vowels; word patterns; and blends. The student's knowledge of words, sentences, punctuation, and other conventions can also be assessed through writing samples.

Figure 6-6 is a writing sample from Stephanie's journal. It is writing she completed independently. This sample provides Mrs. Kurtz with further evidence about what Stephanie knows. She understands beginning and ending sounds and, for the most part, uses them correctly. She also knows several high-frequency words in addition to the ones she demonstrated on the writing vocabulary and dictation assessments: *one, night, little, brother, today, we,* and *but*. Stephanie correctly wrote the *-ing* ending for coming. She is still confused about some medial vowels, as shown in *cuming, weill,* and *slep*. These are confusions Mrs. Kurtz will work on with Stephanie. Mrs. Kurtz will use magnetic letters to practice the correct spelling of the word. She will call attention to those words in reading and ask Stephanie to write those words in sentences.

For a complete discussion of each of the procedures discussed above, see *An Observation Survey of Early Literacy Achievement* by Marie Clay (1993a) and *Guided Reading* by Irene Fountas and Gay Su Pinnell (1996).

Anecdotal Records

Anecdotal records are brief, dated notes of the teacher's observations of students' reading and writing behaviors. Anecdotal records are objective and specific, stating what the student can do. For example, Jose independently wrote *bike* and *game* with the *e* on it. It is the first time he has used the silent *e* without a prompt. These observations present the teacher with a pattern of behaviors and can be used to determine instruction and grouping.

Figure 6-6. Writing Sample

Checklists

Checklists can also provide a teacher with information about students' growth in phonics. Since it is important that the phonics instruction is based on the assessed needs of the students, a checklist prewritten by a publisher will be of little use. The teacher can make a checklist with the students' names down the side of the paper and the phonics activities taught across the top. The teacher can check which students were successful in that activity. Checklists such as these allow the teacher to monitor student needs for instruction. Students who were not successful will need opportunities for more instruction and practice.

Retelling

Although it is important for teachers to monitor and assess student progress in phonics, they will also want to monitor students' comprehension. This can be done through asking students to retell a passage or story they have read. Beginning readers can retell a story they have heard. The teacher can assess the students' understanding of sequence, problem, solution, character, and detail. The goal is that students apply their knowledge of phonics generalizations to understanding what they read. For a complete discussion of retelling, see *Primary Purposes: Assessing* by Fowler and McCullum (1995a), or *Read and Retell* by Brown and Cambourne.

In summary, the teacher can obtain a wealth of information about her students using the assessments described in this section. In addition to demonstrating what the students know and can do, these assessments offer the teacher a window into students' thinking. The teacher can learn as much from errors as from correct responses. A teacher who understands the students' thought processes can plan instruction that maximizes student progress.

Planning Phonics Instruction

As we explained in chapter 2, teaching phonics in a literature-based classroom involves managing a balance of whole-class, small-group, and individualized instruction. The explanation of the following teaching techniques will include which grouping is most appropriate for that technique. Some instructional techniques are appropriate to more than one grouping situation.

Shared Reading

Shared reading is a critical aspect of a balanced approach to literacy instruction. It provides beginning readers with opportunities to read with the teacher, an experienced reader. The teacher's support provides beginning and less-able readers with opportunities for successful reading. In the early grades, the teacher reads from enlarged text, such as big books, and from charts or posters containing poems, finger plays, songs, nursery rhymes, or an interactive story written by the teacher and class. Pointing to the words while reading, the teacher calls children's attention to the relationship between sounds and letters and to conventions of print. Participating in shared reading also builds the children's sight vocabulary. Words that children know automatically can be used to help decode new words. For example, when children know the word *can*, they can change the onset to decode *man, ran, fan.*

During shared reading, the teacher guides and encourages the children's contributions to the reading. The teacher varies the support for the reading of the text while gauging the children's successful contributions. Reading material is chosen to match a purpose based on the teachers' assessments of children's needs. For example, the teacher chooses *Greedy Cat* by Joy Cowley (1991) as a shared reading. This book is chosen to highlight consonant diagraphs for the children. After reading the book with the children, the teacher points out the consonant diagraphs *sh* and *th*, found over and over in this book. Using Wikki Stix™ or a cardboard frame, the children circle these diagraphs with teacher support. Using a cardboard frame, Wikki Stix™, or highlighting tape allows children to physically work with sounds and letters, thus adding a manipulative feature to working with print. This physical manipulation makes sounds and letters more concrete and less abstract for young learners. After the children find the diagraphs, the teacher may ask them to find diagraphs in other books they are reading or in some of the print around the room. For children who seem to have a good grasp on diagraphs, the teacher may ask them to reread *Greedy Cat*, looking for blends and distinguishing them from diagraphs.

As children become more capable readers in second and third grade, shared reading takes on a different form, with the teacher reading from a book while the students follow along in their own copy of the book. A teacher can also choose to put a passage on the overhead projector for a shared reading lesson. Phonics lessons at this level involve structural analysis of words. Students identify inflectional endings, suffixes, and prefixes.

Shared reading is usually conducted with a whole class or small groups of students. However, shared reading can be used with individual students.

Guided Reading

Guided reading requires the students to independently read a book after the teacher introduces it. Guided reading is appropriate for small groups of three to five children or for individual children. In a group, each child has a copy of the book. This is very important for providing independent practice. Teachers choose children to participate in guided reading groups after assessing needs. Children with similar instructional needs are placed in the same group. It is important to note that these groups are flexible, and students do not remain in any one group for an extended period of time. Teachers group and regroup the children according to their progress and their constantly changing needs. The reading material for each group is chosen carefully according to the needs of the group.

Steps in Guided Reading

Determine the purpose for the group's lesson. For example, the teacher might plan a lesson about verbs ending in *-ing*.

Choose a book to match the purpose. A good book for this lesson is *Moonlight* by Marcia Vaughan (1997). This is a little book containing the following verbs: *lighting, watching, playing, shining, sitting, floating,* and *smiling*.

Preview the book to plan an introduction to the book. Note unusual word structures or vocabulary. When using *Moonlight,* the teacher will want to plan a brief discussion about *-ing*.

Introduce the book, being careful to relate the introduction to the purpose of the lesson. First discuss the cover, encouraging predictions. A note of caution: Do not let the students' predictions stray too far from the story line, because some unnecessary or incorrect vocabulary will be put in their heads and will interfere with their reading of the text. For example, in this book the moon is playing, sitting, and so on. The cover and the title of this book do not indicate the actions in the book. This could be confusing for the children, and the teacher will want to guide the predictions accordingly. Always read the title of the book and the author's name. Titles are sometimes difficult and can cause confusion. Giving the children the title of the book will eliminate confusion. *Moonlight* is a good example of a book in which the title and the content of the story do not exactly match.

Talk through the book without reading it. Look at each page and discuss it with the students, using the language found in the text. This is the tricky part. It takes practice to introduce a book by using the structure of the text language but not actually reading the text. A conversational tone should be maintained while putting the vocabulary and language structures into the children's head prior to their independent reading. During the introduction, the teacher may ask students to point to certain words. When using *Moonlight* for teaching *-ing* verbs, the teacher will ask students to point to the words *playing, shining, sitting*. The *-ing* part of the words will be emphasized in the discussion. For a full discussion of book introductions, see "Introducing a New Storybook to Young Readers" by Marie Clay (1991).

Ask students to read the book independently. This can be done as they sit around the teacher, or students can read in other areas of the room. Please note that if students stay in the same area to read, the reading may begin to sound like a choral reading; students should be independently working on the text. The introduction should have provided the students with enough support to read the book and solve problems on their own.

Assess students' success with the reading. This is a time to circulate and listen to the students read, taking anecdotal records on what the students are doing. More-skilled students who read silently can be asked to read a section aloud to determine their progress. This assessment allows the teacher to determine the success of the lesson and plan future lessons.

Return to the text after the students have finished reading. Bring the students back to the group to respond to the reading. Listen to their spontaneous responses first. Ask the students questions about the text, but work to keep the discussion more conversational than the teacher-question, student-answer format. Try to ask questions that encourage the students to make personal connections to an experience in their lives or to prior learning.

Plan one or two teaching opportunities based on the needs of the students. It is best to plan that one of the teaching opportunities will be related to the purpose of the lesson. For the book *Moonlight*, this may mean reteaching *-ing* or revisiting the rhyming words in the book and how the rimes help to make the book easy to read. Do not try to teach more than one or two lessons at this time. More than one or two lessons will be hard for the children to retain.

Ask students to respond to the text. This may be done in a variety of ways. Rereading is one of the best responses. When students reread, they practice the skills taught and build fluency. Rereading provides students with much-needed practice and rehearsal of reading. It allows them to consolidate new learning with prior learning about reading. Other ways to respond to reading is by writing, dramatizing, or creating artwork about a reading selection. Students can also read related literature by the same author or on the same topic.

Writing

Writing provides students with another way to develop and practice phonics skills. Student writing samples demonstrate what phonics skills students know and can apply. Writing is the meaningful context in which children practice the application of their understandings about sound—letter matching, sound segmentation, onsets and rimes, and sound manipulation. In Figure 6-7, children used technology to create rime families.

Figure 6-7. Rime Families

The following kinds of writing experiences describe different ways that teachers can help children to learn about sounds and letters and how to apply that knowledge to both writing and reading.

Shared Writing

In shared writing, the teacher and students write together. The teacher acts as scribe, writing text large enough for all the students to see while thinking aloud to demonstrate how writing is talk written down. Students are asked to contribute words, individual letters, and clusters of letters, including endings, as the message is composed. Shared writing can be used with the whole class, small groups, or with individual children. Shared writing includes morning messages, class news, a group story, or other experiences the teacher and class want to record.

In the early part of the year, especially in the lower grades, the teacher composes and writes the message. As the student's skills progress, the students contribute to the actual writing. In the beginning, the teacher may compose a message leaving out letters. The omissions in the message are determined by the students' needs. Very early in the year, a first-grade teacher will omit beginning letters. As the students progress, the teacher may omit ending letters, medial vowels, rimes, or inflectional endings. The following is an example of a morning message the teacher wrote early in the year before the children came to school. Together the teacher and children determine the missing letters.

> Good __orning,
>
> Today is __onday. We will have __usic today.
> The weather is warm. We __ay go outside for recess.
>
> Love,
>
> ____iss Parker

Miss Parker will help the children to decide what letter should go in the blanks. She might also point out the *m* at the end of *warm*. Depending on the class, she and the students might also add some sentences containing words with the letter *m*.

Another way to conduct shared reading is by composing the message with the students and thinking aloud. In this case, the teacher might write *Good* and then say, "The next word is *morning*. Who knows what letter *morning* starts with?" As the writing progresses, the teacher continues to ask students about letters they know. Later in the year, the teacher asks the children to write some of the letters and words in the message. As the teacher and children write, the children learn about beginning and ending sounds, medial vowels, blends, diagraphs, and inflectional endings. The teacher plans the message to teach these skills.

Students in second and third grade can compose shared messages without the teacher doing the writing. The teacher can use these messages to work on the structure of words and spelling. After the students have written the message, the teacher and students can check for correct spelling, and the teacher can provide a lesson on spelling generalizations when correcting misspellings.

Interactive Writing

During interactive writing, the teacher and the students work together to compose a message. It is a powerful technique for teaching phonics, as students and teacher work on the sounds in each word. Interactive writing also helps beginning readers to attend to the details of print, such as left-to-right progression, spaces between words, and punctuation. During interactive writing, both teacher and students use the pencil or marker. When the class is involved in independent reading and writing tasks, it is a good time for the teacher to work individually with one student or with a small group of students for 5–10 minutes on interactive writing (Fowler & McCallum, 1995c). The following steps for interactive writing provide students with support in developing and applying knowledge of phonics skills.

Gather the group of students in a place where they can see the easel or chart paper. When working with an individual student, sit beside the student.

Ask the children to orally compose a sentence. This allows the students to see that writing makes sense and that thoughts and ideas can be written and re-read. The teacher writes the sentence in a place separate from where the children will write the sentence. In this way, the teacher can help the students if a word or the sentence is forgotten.

Ask the children to say the first word slowly, stretching out the sounds. If the children have difficulty stretching out the word slowly, use a rubber band and stretch it out as the children say the word.

Prompt the children with questions about what they can contribute to the writing. These questions mostly focus on the sounds in words. Examples of questions to ask are as follows:

What do you hear when you say____?

What else do you hear?

What letter do you expect to make that sound?

How many sounds do you hear?

Do you remember how to write_____?

Ask the children what the first letter of the first word is. Invite a child to write as many letters of the word as possible. When the child does not know a letter, ask the other children to help. If the students cannot determine the next letter(s), the teacher writes the letter. The teacher does not write any parts of the word that the child can do on his or her own. For example, the child wants to write the word *spider*.

Child: It starts with *s*. (*The teacher gives the child the marker to write the* s *and then takes the marker back.*)

Teacher: What else do you hear in the word *spider*? Say it slowly.

Child (*saying the word slowly*): *S-p-i-d-e-r*. I hear a *p*.

Teacher: That's right. *P* is the next letter. (*She gives the marker back to the child, who writes* p.) What do you hear next?

Child: *S-p-i-d-e-r. i.*

Teacher: That's right. Go ahead and write the *i* next to the *p*. What else do you hear?

Child: *S-p-i-d-e-r. d, r.*

Teacher: There is a *d* next, but there is another letter before the *r*. Go ahead and write the *d*. (*After the child writes the* d, *the teacher takes the marker and asks the other students what letter they think comes next.*)

Another child: *e*

Teacher: Yes, it is an *e*.

The teacher writes an *e*, explaining that it is hard to hear but that the *e* comes before the *r*. The teacher returns the marker to the student to write the *r*.

Continue this process until the entire sentence is written. Other students are invited to write the words and letters they know with the teacher filling in the unknown letters. The teacher and children exchange the marker as necessary. If a child writes an incorrect letter, the teacher covers the error with correction tape. Correction tape is used rather than an eraser because correction tape provides a clean, untorn product. It also requires less effort, and the children will focus less on fixing errors than correct writing.

Repeat the sentence orally before writing each word so the meaning of the sentence is maintained.

Provide the children with time to read the sentence when the writing is complete.

At the completion of the session, the teacher and children have written one or two sentences with correct spelling, spacing, capitalization, and punctuation. These sentences provide a correct model of print for emerging readers and writers.

When working with an individual child, the teacher can make a copy of the sentence for the child to practice reading. She can also provide the sentence in cut-up form so that the students can practice putting the sentence in order.

For group lessons, the teacher and children may add to the story over several days, giving each child in the group a chance to contribute a sentence to the story or message. Each day, before starting to write the new sentence, the teacher and children reread the previous sentence(s) to maintain the meaning. As when working with individual students, teachers can cut up sentences or stories for the group of children to practice putting in sequence.

As stated previously, interactive writing is a powerful tool for helping children to learn and apply phonics to solving words in both reading and writing.

Innovations on Text

Innovations on text are when the teacher and students produce a piece of writing that is based on a patterned, familiar story. These innovations provide the teacher with opportunities to examine the details of the text carefully while reinforcing phonics skills. The completed innovations can be added to the class library, and the students enjoy reading and rereading them. As students reread the texts, they practice fluency and build their bank of known words. *Rosie's Walk* by Pat Hutchins (1983) lends itself to innovations. The teacher and class can have Rosie walk around, past, over, or under any number of places different from those in the book.

Children also enjoy creating innovations on *Where's Spot?* by Eric Hill (1980). They especially like having innovations based on themselves, such as "Where's Jose?" or "Where's Stephanie?" Books like *Katie Did It* by Becky McDaniel (1983) and *Just Like Grandpa* by Cheryl Semple and Judy Tuer (1997) provide models for innovations. As students become more skilled writers, they can write their own innovations with less teacher guidance.

Independent Writing

Students need opportunities to write independently about topics they choose. Independent writing provides opportunities for students to practice the skills they have learned. Teachers encourage children to write in a variety of forms, including stories, reports, notes, letters, invitations, lists, charts, and journals. All writing that is posted for public view should exhibit correct spelling, capitalization, and punctuation. Writing that is displayed must provide a correct model for the students.

Spelling

Student writing is often filled with misspellings. Teachers can view these errors as a way to determine what the learner knows about sounds, letters, suffixes, prefixes, inflectional endings, and spelling generalizations. Observing the students' errors helps to guide the teacher's instruction. Children need opportunities to attempt unknown words. These temporary spellings are the students' attempts to find order in the spelling system. If children do not have opportunities to write unknown words, it is difficult to teach to their needs (Bolton & Snowball, 1993b).

Learning to spell develops in stages. Gentry (1982) defined spelling stages as precommunicative, semiphonetic, phonetic, traditional, and correct. Children progress through these stages, but this does not mean that they cannot be expected to spell high-frequency words correctly. Children in the phonetic stage match the essential letters and sounds but may omit medial vowels or hard-to-hear consonants, such as the *n* in *went* or the *n* in the *-ing* ending. They may also substitute soundalike letters in words e.g., *kat* (cat), *cnak* (snake), *plez* (please).

At the same time these children are spelling words like *in, at,* and *like* correctly. As children progress to the transitional stage, they put vowels in every syllable; they use the silent *e* correctly or sometimes overgeneralize, such as *shepe*; they use inflectional endings correctly; they may use the correct letters but in the incorrect sequence, such as *becuase*; vowel diagraphs appear, such as *caik* or *cayk*. In this stage, more known or correctly spelled words appear frequently. At the correct stage of spelling, students have learned and correctly apply spelling generalizations. They also have a large body of known words they correctly spell in their writing.

Teachers need to understand these stages so they can assess their students' knowledge of phonics, spelling, and conventions of print. Creating an environment where students feel confident to attempt unknown words will yield writing that allows the teacher to have valuable knowledge of what students know and need to learn. The teacher's goal is for the students to spell conventionally, and these expectations must be conveyed to students while continuing to provide a safe environment for the exploration of words.

CHAPTER 7

Developing
 Word Recognition Skills
and Strategies

Word recognition is the term used most frequently to define the processes readers use to identify a word. Adams (1990) states "that skillful word recognition involves both visual processing and phonological translation" (p. 105). The goal of instruction in word recognition is to help the reader develop an ever-expanding pool of words that can be recognized instantaneously. These words are recognized in isolation and within context. In addition to recognition of whole words, readers develop recognition of recurring letter combinations within words, such as the rimes listed in chapter 6, prefixes, suffixes, and inflectional endings. Once a reader recognizes sight words and common word parts, less effort is required for distinguishing the actual words, and more effort can be directed toward understanding the meaning of the words (Pressley, 1998). Building a bank of sight words is critical to developing fluency. Readers who are forced to concentrate on decoding each word have difficulty understanding what they read. Automaticity in word recognition assists the reader in maintaining comprehension while reading.

Sight Words

Teachers generally have three understandings of the term *sight words*. The first understanding is those words children come to school reading, such as their names, *McDonald's*, or *Burger King*. These words have not been taught to the students. The second understanding is those words that appear frequently in all text and are essential to fluent reading. These words are sometimes referred to as *glue words* because they hold text together (Wagstaff, 1994). Adams (1990) lists the 150 most frequent words printed in English. Some of these words are soundable and others do not follow sound patterns. Wagstaff (1994) used a list composed of words that do not follow patterns to teach her students. Those words include the following:

a	*of*	*they*	*where*
again	*one*	*through*	*which*
any	*people*	*to*	*who*
are	*said*	*two*	*with*
because	*some*	*use*	*you*
been	*the*	*very*	*your*
do	*their*	*was*	
have	*there*	*were*	
many	*these*	*what*	

Examples of soundable high frequency words are: *and, in, is, it, at, an, man, can, him, did.* There are a variety of high-frequency word lists that teachers can use and adapt to the needs of their students. In teaching children who are English as a Second Language (ESL) learners, teachers find a need to include prepositions such as *over, on, under, by,* and *around* on our sight word lists. A third understanding teachers have of sight words are those words needed to understand a topic or concept within a school subject. These words are vocabulary words introduced to students to assist in comprehending a reading selection. Generally these words are content related. Some examples include family titles, such as *mother, father, sister, brother, aunt, uncle;* or words representing less familiar concepts, such as *colony, pilgrim, explorer, ancient,* or *civilization.*

Environmental Print

As stated previously, children come to school recognizing words, such as *McDonald's, stop, Pepsi.* This is called *logographic reading,* and while not real reading, it plays a part in reading development (Pressley, 1998). Young children notice print in their environment, and these encounters with print provide children with knowledge of words and the functions of language. Environmental print helps children to understand that words are useful and communicate meaning (Hall, 1987). By providing a print-rich environment in the classroom, teachers can enrich children's awareness of print, words, and functions of written language. According to Cambourne (1988), immersion is a necessary condition for learning. Teachers plan for developing word recognition skills by filling their classrooms with print and building upon their students' prior knowledge of words. Taking a neighborhood walk can provide a teacher with a wealth of resources for teaching sight words. In the beginning of first grade, Mrs. Irwin takes her class for a walk around the neighborhood. She uses a Polaroid or QuickTake camera to record pictures of the environmental print her students identify, such as *stop, Seven Eleven, Post Office, Rite Aid,* and *library.* Mrs. Irwin chooses some other print to record, such as the school name, library, cafeteria, and office. She and her students glue these pictures into a book. Mrs. Irwin then reads as a shared reading this book and other books, such as *I Walk and Read* (1984), *I Read Symbols* (1988), and *I Read Signs* (1987) by Tana Hoban. Through repeated readings, Mrs. Irwin's students learn to recognize many of the words. Another environmental print activity Mrs. Irwin uses involves the children bringing words from their home environment that they can recognize. These words are usually found on cereal boxes, magazines like *TV Guide*, milk cartons, and other products. The students and Mrs. Irwin talk about these words, noticing the letters they start with, the letters they end with, and the word parts. Mrs. Irwin and the students glue these words to magnetic strips and put them on a metal heating system in the room. A magnetic cookie sheet also works. The children investigate and manipulate these words during reading and writing activity times.

Teaching by Analogy to Known Words

Teachers like Mrs. Irwin build on this knowledge of environmental print by instructing the children in using known words to determine new words. This is called teaching by analogy. Research by Goswami & Bryant (1990) indicates that readers use known words to figure out unfamiliar words. If the reader comes to the unknown word *pride*, that reader can use the known word *ride* to pronounce *pride*. Often teachers start building on analogies by using the students' knowledge of the names of the children in the class. If the children can identify Stephanie's name, they can use that knowledge to identify the *st* in *stop* and *stack*. Students can practice this recognition first by sorting the names of the children into lists of those names that start the same. Teachers put the names on cards so children can easily manipulate the names as they sort. Figure 7-1 shows names sorted by the beginning letter. Later other words are added and sorted, as shown in Figure 7-2. In addition to sorting by the onsets of words, children can sort words according to rimes (Figure 7-3).

Teachers follow up on the sorting by asking the children to use individual white boards or chalkboards to write the words.

> **Mrs. Sens** (*after gathering a group of children and distributing white boards and markers*): Write the word *back*.
>
> *Students write the word on the boards while Mrs. Sens makes a quick visual check to see if the word is correctly spelled.*
>
> **Mrs. Sens:** Change the first letter to make the word *sack*. What letter will you use?
>
> **Students:** *S.* (*They quickly erase the* b *and change it to an* s.)
>
> **Mrs. Sens:** Let's change the word to *tack*. What letter will we use?
>
> **Students:** *T.* (*They again erase and change the first letter.*)

Figure 7-1. Names Sorted by First Letter

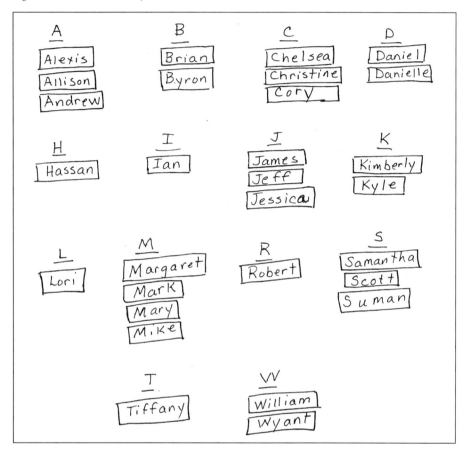

Figure 7-2. Words Added to First-Letter Sort

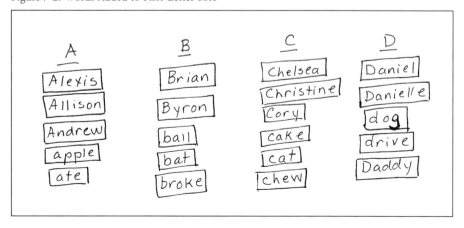

Figure 7-3. Words Sorted by Rime

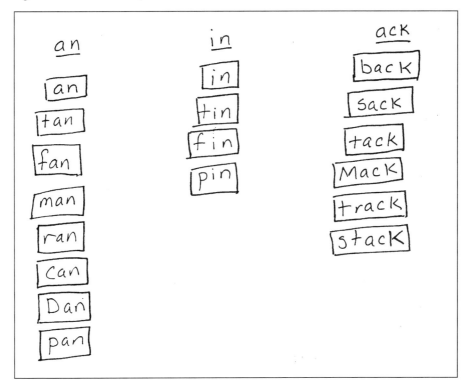

Mrs. Sens can ask the children to suggest letters to make words. Depending on her students, she can ask them to change the word using consonant blends or diagraphs. This activity reinforces the children's knowledge of the word part -*ack*. When they encounter -*ack* in their reading, they apply that knowledge to determining the unknown word.

Using individual white boards or chalkboards provides the children the opportunity to practice and apply their learning in a format that allows them to work quickly, erasing and rewriting more easily than can be accomplished with paper and pencil. This practice helps students to build fluency with the words. In addition, the teacher can quickly assess students' work and make decisions about what to teach next and which students need extra help. Recording this information in anecdotal notes or on a checklist helps the teacher to recall student learning behaviors and assists in the planning of instruction for individual students.

Word Walls

Teachers ask children to sort words according to a variety of other categories. See Figure 7-4. Sorting words allows students to study the features of words, to compare and contrast words, and to classify words into categories. Children form and test hypotheses about words and develop an understanding of the generalizations that apply to the letters and sounds in words (Pinnell & Fountas, 1998).

Figure 7-4. Suggested Categories for Sorting Words

Sorting According to Letters and Sounds

- Words that begin with the same letter
- Words that begin with consonant blends
- Words that begin with consonant clusters
- Words that end with consonant clusters
- Words that end with the same rime
- Words with double consonants
- Words with the same vowel sound as *apple*
- Words with the same vowel sound as *egg*
- Words with the same beginning vowel sound as *igloo*
- Words with the same beginning vowel sound as *octopus*
- Words with the same beginning vowel sound as *umbrella*
- Words with the same vowel sound as *take*
- Words with the same vowel sound as *meet*
- Words with the same vowel sound as *like*
- Words with the same vowel sound as *boat*
- Words with the same vowel sound as *cute*
- Words with a silent *e*
- Word with *r* controlled vowels

Sorting According to Structure and Meaning

- Words with prefixes
- Words with suffixes
- Words with the same root words
- Words that are compounds
- Words that are action words
- Words that describe
- Words that are homophones
- Words that are contractions
- Words with inflectional endings
- Words that are plural

As students sort words, these words are placed in the determined categories on a word wall. The word wall provides a useful resource for continued word study. As children discover words fitting the categories in their reading and writing, they continue to add words to the categories on the wall. The teacher assesses the students' progress in different categories. As students become skilled in applying the different categories, the teacher and students determine which categories to eliminate. Other categories are added as the teacher determines needs. The teacher can assess students by asking them to write words using the patterns in the categories. For example, Mrs. Parker has a group of students gather in front of the word wall. The children and Mrs. Parker review a category she thinks the students have mastered. The category is "words that contain an *a* with a silent *e*." Mrs. Parker has a list of words that fit this pattern but are not on the wall. She dictates these words to the children, who write them using paper on a clipboard. Mrs. Parker and the children check their success after writing the words. Mrs. Parker determines the children have a good understanding of this pattern and removes this category from the word wall.

The word wall can also be used to play games like *I Spy* or *Twenty Questions*. The teacher first models how to play but can later release the clue-giving role to the children. For example, the following clues can be given.

I spy a word on the word wall that:

- starts with *p*
- has a silent *e*
- has two letters that are the same in the middle
- has three letters that stand up higher than the others
- follows the double consonant *-le* pattern

The children guess after each clue. This activity causes children to attend to features of print, word patterns, sounds, and letters.

Twenty Questions is played by the teacher or one child selecting a word from the word wall. The other children ask yes or no questions about the word. The number of questions can vary. It could be 5 or 10 questions, depending on the difficulty of the words on the wall and the skill of the children. The children can work in teams to determine the selected words. Children are encouraged to ask questions related to the patterns and features of the word rather than asking the exact letters. Questions include:

- Does it have more than one syllable?
- Does it have more than one vowel?
- Does it have any double letters?
- Does it have a prefix or suffix?
- Does it have any silent letters?

After studying words and patterns, children will generate many more questions.

Games like *I Spy* and *Twenty Questions* cause children to scan the features of print, develop a knowledge of letters, make connections concerning clusters of letters and letter patterns, and refine language for talking about words.

Words on the wall can be organized in webs showing the connections be-tween the meanings of words. See Figure 7-5 for an example. Seeing the connec-tions of words based on meaning is helpful to children as they build their banks of known words. Questions about the meanings of words on the word walls can be added to the *Twenty Questions* and *I Spy* games. Children then connect the visual features of words to their meanings and strengthen their knowledge of those words.

Figure 7-5. Connections Between Word Meanings

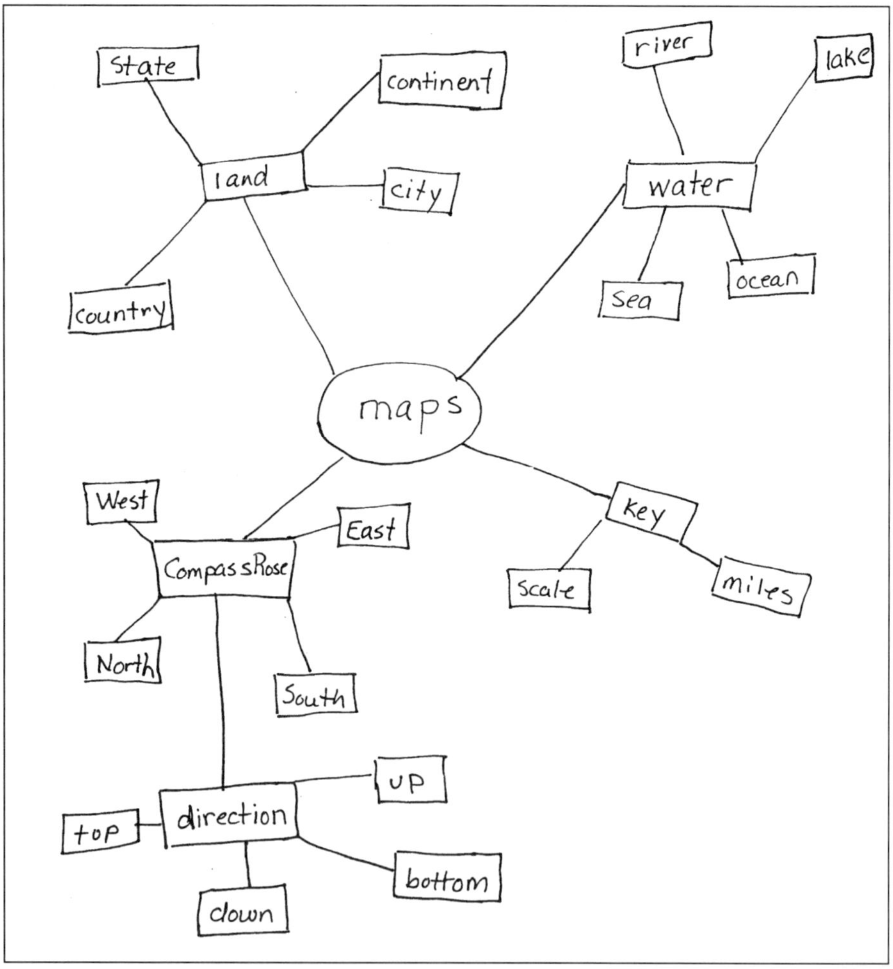

Reading the Room

Reading the room is an activity that gives students the opportunity to practice reading words that have been introduced and discussed during direct instruction. Teachers furnish a supply of interesting pointers for the children to use as they read. Reading in pairs provides students with partners who can check the correct reading of words, and each child is pointing to the word being read. Working together, children can solve problems and identify the words in the room. Teachers sometimes provide paper for the children to record the words they are reading in the room. This works best when the children are looking for specific patterns and recording them on a chart or web. For example, the teacher might ask the children reading the room to find words with the double consonant -*le* pattern. As children become more skilled in reading the room for specific patterns, the teacher asks them to find more than one pattern as they read the room. Teachers also ask children to categorize words in the room. The children sort and record words they can read into categories such as words with a long *o*, words with a silent *e*, or words with more than three syllables. These written sheets provide the teacher with assessment information. He or she can determine if the students can recognize and categorize words with similar patterns. Lessons are planned for students demonstrating difficulty. The teacher can also assess students by observing them as they read the room. This information is recorded in anecdotal records.

Reading the room provides opportunities to develop fluency and automaticity in word recognition and to apply learned skills to solve problems in word recognition. It also allows young children to move around while reading, using pointers such as apples on sticks, curly sticks, or bejeweled sticks. The novel pointers and movement meet the physical needs of young learners while enhancing their experiences with reading words.

Making Words

Making words (Cunningham & Hall, 1994) is an activity that provides children with an opportunity to manipulate letters to make words. Students are given a predetermined set of letters that when put together make one longer word. As a warm-up, the teacher asks the children to make a two-letter word, then another two-letter word, then three-letter words, and so on until the children use all the letters to make the big word. According to Cunningham and Hall (1994), making words is a multilevel, manipulative activity that provides "endless possibilities for discovering how our alphabetic system works" (p. 1).

To prepare for making words, Mrs. Quinn makes sets of letter cards with lower case letters on one side and uppercase on the other. Vowels are done in red or another contrasting color. The children learn that every word must have one vowel in it. Mrs. Quinn also has a set of large letters to use with the pocket chart. As Mrs. Quinn prepares for a making words lesson, she chooses the long word *crickets* from the current science unit. She writes a list of all the small words that can be made. Mrs. Quinn writes these words on index cards and puts them in order from smallest to largest. She then determines what pattern or patterns she wants to emphasize. Figure 7-6 shows Mrs. Quinn's word list.

Mrs. Quinn gathers a group of children around her. She likes to conduct making words lessons with small groups of children so she can tie the word patterns to the demonstrated learning needs of the children and easily observe their

Figure 7-6. Mrs. Quinn's Words

```
it
is
sit
kit
kite
sick
tick
kick
Rick
crick
cricket
crickets
```

work. Mrs. Quinn gives the children their sets of letters, and she displays hers on the pocket chart. She asks the students to make a two-letter word. She writes the numeral *2* on her white board and holds up two fingers. She says, "I am thinking of the word *is*. Who can make *is*? It is sunny today." Using the letter cards the children make *is*. Mrs. Quinn asks them to make another two-letter word. "Who can make *it*? He will do it." She asks children to make the two-letter words in the pocket chart. She displays the index cards with the two-letter words on them in the pocket chart. She then asks the children to make three-letter words. She writes the numeral *3* and holds up three fingers. She asks the children to make *sit*, then *set*. She makes sure to use the words in a sentence. When Mrs. Quinn gets to four-letter words, she includes *Rick* as one of the words. She checks to see that the students use a capital *R* to begin the name. She helps students who did not use the capital letter to remember that proper names begin with capital letters. Mrs. Quinn continues this method until the long word *crickets* is made. Mrs. Quinn has chosen to emphasize the *-ick* pattern. She asks the students to write the *-ick* words quickly on their white boards. She asks them to make other *-ick* words. In this way, she can check to see who can apply their learning to other words. For a complete discussion of procedures, see the book *Making Words* by Cunningham and Hall.

Word Play

Word play is an enjoyable way for students to practice skills. They can apply knowledge of sounds and letters, onsets and rimes, features of print, and word meanings.

Chants, Rhymes, Poems, and Songs

Reciting chants, rhymes, and poems and singing songs builds students' sensitivity to the sounds of language. When the reciting and singing is accompanied by reading the text, the students increase the number of words they recognize. Children delight in alliteration and rhyme, and they relish saying phrases such as "angry alligators all around" and "Dan, Dan, the flying man."

The following chant is an example of a way in which teachers and students can play with words while consolidating rhyming words as known words and developing flexibility in recognizing words.

> The teacher and students read together:
> If I can read . . .
> The teacher writes the word *Ben,* a student in the class.
> The students read with the teacher:
> If I can read *Ben,* then I can read . . .
> The teacher writes the word *pen.*
> The students and teacher read together:
> If I can read *Ben,* then I can read *pen.* If I can read *pen,* then I can read . . .
> The teacher writes the word *hen.*
> The students read:
> If I can read *hen,* then I can read . . .
> The teacher writes the word *pen.*
> The students read:
> If I can read *hen,* then I can read *pen.* If I can read *pen,* then I can read . . .
> The teacher writes the word *men.*
> The students read:
> If I can read *pen,* then I can read *men.*

After a list of words that have the same rime is compiled on the board or a chart, the teacher and students reread the chant quickly. As students progress, more difficult onsets and rimes are used; for example, "If I can read *lend,* then I can read friend." This activity causes students to use their knowledge of onsets and rimes and builds automatic word recognition. Children can also use their knowledge of the chanted words to problem solve decoding new words.

Word Stairs, Word Ladders, Word Searches, and Crosswords

These word play activities promote thinking about letters and words. When completing these activities, students consider what words look like and the correct spelling. Working on these kinds of activities increases word recognition and develops flexible thinking.

Word stairs help students to see similarities in words, explore the features of words, and problem solve about words. A word stair is built by using the last letter of one word to start the next word, as shown in Figure 7-7. Teachers often provide graph paper to help students make their word stairs.

Figure 7-7. Word Stair

A word ladder is another activity to promote students' thinking flexibility about words and letters while building word recognition. To make a word ladder, start with a word, then change one or two letters to make a new word. This continues until the student(s) cannot think of any more words. Allowing students to change only one letter makes this a more challenging activity. Figure 7-8 shows a word ladder built when only one letter could be changed.

Word searches are words arranged horizontally, vertically, and diagonally within a grid of letters. Students are to find and circle words. A list of words the students are to find can be provided, or students can search for as many words as they can find in the grid. There are many commercially made word searches available. However, children enjoy making word searches. The teacher can provide graph paper for the students to use when making word searches. Students can use words from units of study to reinforce the recognition of vocabulary.

Crossword puzzles furnish students with practice in recognizing words and understanding meaning. Students can make their own puzzles using graph paper or one of the computer programs on the market that generate crossword puzzles. Making a challenging crossword puzzle for fellow classmates is an engaging activity for many students. Students can use letter tiles as they create their crossword puzzles.

Figure 7-8. Word Ladder

at
bat
sat
sit
site
bite
bit
bin
fin
fine
find
Kind

Manipulating Letters and Words

Providing students with opportunities to make word recognition a physical, manipulative activity builds strength in word recognition skills. In addition to the activities listed, teachers arrange for students to use magnetic letters and letter tiles to make words. These tools enable students to quickly make and change words. For example, children choose the letters to make the word *take*, then change the onset letter from *t* to *m*, spelling *make*. *Make* can easily be changed to *fake*, then to *bake, rake, brake*, etc. Physically moving premade letters is easier than writing the letters for many beginning learners. When the students read books with common rimes, the teacher helps them to identify those rimes by making connections to the letter manipulation activities. Noting that a book contains the words *sand, band,* and *land,* the teacher models by covering the beginning letter of the first of these words that appears in the text and asking the students to say the rime. The teacher and the students look for the next word that has the same rime and identify both the new onset and the rime. The teacher reminds the children that this is similar to when they moved the letter tiles to change onsets and make new words. Again, flexibility and automaticity is being developed by using manipulatives and relating the concrete activity to the more abstract reading work in the text.

Teachers also make recognizing words and word parts physical by using Wikki Stix™, Post-its™, and highlighter tape. Teachers and children use Wikki Stix™ to circle words, onsets, rimes, prefixes, suffixes, and inflectional endings on the page in a big book or on a chart. Words and word parts on large text can be masked using Post-its™. The teacher asks the children to predict what the word might be based on the context, beginning letter(s), or ending letter(s) depending on the needs of the children. Early in the year, first grade teacher Miss Huestis uses the book *Mrs. Wishy-Washy* by Joy Cowley (1990) for a shared reading. She and the children have read it before. This time, Miss Huestis has covered the verbs describing the animals' actions with Post-it™ Notes. She leaves the first letter of the word showing so the children can use the beginning letter as a clue to determine the word when they read the book. As the children progress, Miss Huestis uses the same book with highlighter tape to teach the *-ed* inflectional ending. Highlighter tape is clear vinyl tape that can be purchased in different colors. When placed on a word or word part, the letters show through the tape. Materials such as Wikki Stix™, Post-its™, and highlighter tape assist students in visually attending to letters and words.

Reading and Rereading

Word recognition is supported by shared reading, guided reading, and independent reading. The more children read, the more words they recognize. During shared reading of enlarged text, teachers point to the words as they say them, helping beginning readers to see the relationship between the spoken and written words. As students participate in guided reading lessons, teachers use the techniques and activities described in this book that are designed to help students recognize words.

Teachers choose books for students that support word recognition. Books containing repeated patterns such as those found in *Have You Seen My Cat?* by Eric Carle (1991), *The Cat on the Mat* by Brian Wildsmith (1982), or *The Meanies* by Joy Cowley (1983) allow students to practice the same words over and over while reading. This practice builds automatic word recognition. As children progress, the books chosen become more sophisticated while still providing repeated patterns. These books include titles like *Noisy Nora* by Rosemary Wells (1973) or *I Was Walking Down the Road* by Sara Barchas (1993). Many publishing companies such as Rigby and The Wright Group specialize in publishing pattern books for beginning readers.

Rereading familiar books is critical to developing word recognition and fluency. As children reread books, they consolidate the skills they have learned. Sometimes, children's rereadings appear to be memorization, and children frequently reread old favorites to the point of being able to recite them. This is not cause for alarm. As children reread, they are putting words into their memories. These words can quickly be retrieved when encountered in a new text. Teachers can allay parental worries about rereading by explaining its value. Providing time for rereading in school and sending familiar books home with students will strengthen word recognition.

Vocabulary Development

Word recognition is part of vocabulary development. Students can decode and recognize words without entirely grasping their meanings. To understand words, students must encounter them repeatedly in a variety of texts; this requires time to read as well as reading widely. Oral language and direct instruction do not account for the bulk of a child's vocabulary development; citing a number of studies, Cunningham & Stanovich (1998) states that "many researchers are convinced that reading volume, rather than oral language, is the prime contributor to individual differences in children's vocabularies" (p. 9). The reason for believing that reading in quantity contributes to vocabulary development stems from studies of the differences in word distribution between text and oral language. Hayes and Aherns (1988) analyzed words from different contexts using a standard frequency count of English (Carroll, Davies, & Richman, 1971). In this standard, words are ranked according to how often they appear in written English. Figure 7-9 (adapted from Stanovich, 1998) shows the richness of the vocabulary in children's books as compared to adult conversation.

Figure 7-9. Differences Between Spoken and Written Language

Type of Language	Rank of Median Word	Rare Words per 1000
Children's Books	627	30.9
Preschool books	578	16.3
Conversation—adult college student	496	17.3

Adapted from Cunningham & Stanovich (1998)

A rare word is defined as a word ranked lower than 10,000, or a word that would not be in the vocabulary of a 10- to 12-year old (Stanovich, 1998). Figure 7-9 dramatically demonstrates the differences between written and oral language.

Another study supporting the theory that large amounts of reading increases vocabulary was one by Anderson, Wilson, and Fielding (1988). Although the students in this study were in fifth grade, the implications for younger children are obvious. Anderson et al. found that students who read 0.1 minutes a day outside of school read 8,000 words per year. Compare that to students who read 21.1 minutes a day, who read 1,823,000 words per year. Students who read approximately 1 hour a day read more than 4,000,000 words per year. The correlation of reading volume to vocabulary development cannot be denied.

Assessing Word Recognition

Formal assessment of word recognition can be conducted in a number of ways, several of which were described in chapter 6. Teachers can ask students to read word lists, write known words, and take running records. All of these assessments will furnish the teacher with information about students' word recognition knowledge. Teachers can also informally assess children using checklists and anecdotal records to record information as students read the room, participate in guided reading and shared reading groups, buddy read, and write independently or with others. These assessments will help teachers to make decisions about what instructional techniques for word recognition will most benefit students.

CHAPTER 8

Learning About the

Structural Analysis

of Words

Structural analysis is the study of meaningful word elements, or morphemes. *Morphemes* are the smallest units of meaning in a language, and in English there are thousands of morphemes. Morphemes include words that stand alone, such as *move*, and word parts that cannot stand alone as words—prefixes such as *re-* and suffixes such as *-ing*. While reading *Aunt Chip and the Great Triple Creek Dam Affair* (Polacco, 1996), Kelly, a third-grade student, was delighted to use what she had recently learned about prefixes and suffixes to recognize the words *rebuilding* and *remodeling*. The purpose of learning about structural analysis is to assist readers in determining unfamiliar words by examining the familiar and meaningful parts of those words (Johnson & Pearson, 1984). Kelly easily recognizes the words *build* and *model*. She also knows the *-ing* ending and applies her new knowledge of the prefix *re-* to put the parts together to read the less familiar words.

Structural analysis is another important skill for helping readers to determine and not guess wildly at new words encountered when reading. Teachers introduce structural analysis after students recognize a core of known words and are beginning to understand the meaning relationships between words. In first grade, teachers begin to introduce some concepts of structural analysis, such as the endings *-s*, *-ed*, *-ing*, and contractions. In second and third grade, the focus on structural analysis becomes more intense and concentrates on more sophisticated morphemes, including the meanings of prefixes, suffixes, and derivatives. When teaching about structural analysis, teachers can differentiate instruction to meet the needs of students from struggling to gifted learners. For example, teachers can offer different practice opportunities for learners, including reading, writing, games, and word puzzles.

The teaching of structural analysis is best conducted within the context of reading. Many practice activities are offered in this chapter, but it is important to remember that students will learn best how to apply their knowledge of structural analysis if the teacher demonstrates recognizing and analyzing morphemes during shared reading. It is critical that students have the opportunity to practice identifying word parts within their own independent reading. This independent reading is done with books that are the appropriate reading level for the student to read fluently with understanding. In order to practice new skills, students need to read books that are not frustrating for them. As students study structural analysis, they learn about derivatives, prefixes, suffixes, inflectional endings, and compound words.

Derivatives

Derivatives are words that come from other languages. Knowing about derivatives can be useful to readers in deducing meaning and building vocabulary. In choosing what derivatives to introduce to young children, consider those that are consistent and most useful to the students. For example, when a student recognizes that the word *aqua* means "water," then it is not so difficult to figure out the word *aquarium*. The following is a list of derivatives adapted from a more extensive list in Bolton and Snowball (1993b). The list below represents words that are useful in helping young readers to determine some difficult or challenging words that might be encountered in their reading. It is not intended that these words be memorized. Teaching activities are suggested following the list.

Derivative	Meaning	Example	Origin
aqua	water	aquarium, aquatics	Greek/Latin
audio	to hear	auditorium	Latin
auto	self	automatic	Greek
bios	life	biography	Greek
centum	one hundred	centimeter	Latin
civis	citizen	civics	Latin
cyclos	wheel	bicycle	Greek
deca	ten	decade	Greek
dentis	tooth	dentist	Latin
geo	earth	geography	Greek
grapho	I write	autograph	Greek
metron	measure	meter	Greek
mille	one thousand	millimeter	Greek
octo	eight	octopus	Greek/Latin
pedi	foot	centipede	Latin
penta	five	pentagon	Greek
phono	sound, voice	telephone	Greek
quattor	four	quadrangle	Latin
scope	to view	telescope	Greek
semi	half	semicircle	Latin
tele	from a distance	telephone	Greek

Activities

When planning a shared reading lesson, teachers choose derivatives contained within the text to introduce to students. As derivatives are introduced, teachers write them on chart paper. These charts are hung in the room as resources for the students. Students can classify and sort derivatives according to the way they end or to their origin. Working with derivatives in this way will help children with the meaning and in recognizing derivatives when reading. Students can find as many words as possible containing a derivative. This can be done using a dictionary, trade books, magazines, and newspapers. For example, Mrs. Rogers assigns derivatives to groups of third-grade students. The groups then find as many words as they can that contain that derivative. They are also to note where they found the word. Mrs. Rogers allows the students to work on this task in class and as homework. In this way, parents are involved. The lists are amassed and kept in a class book. Students using the derivative *scope* found *telescope, stethoscope, microscope, radarscope,* and *horoscope* in the dictionary and newspaper.

Students can make word searches containing derivatives. These words can be chosen from their own independent reading, from class charts and books, and from units of study in science and social studies. As children read independently, they can note derivatives found in their reading. These words can be written on Post-its™, and the teacher and children can discuss the meaning of the word, how to classify it, and on what chart the word belongs.

Games are another way to reinforce knowledge of derivatives. The students and teacher can make games like *Bingo, Go Fish,* and *Memory*. Directions for making and playing *Bingo* follow.

Directions for Bingo

Object: Be the first player to complete a row either vertically or diagonally on the playing board. Rows are completed by matching derivatives on the board with those called.

Players: Any number

Materials: A piece of paper with 12 squares for each player
A list of 12 words for the players to place on their papers
Markers for each player

Method of play

Step 1: Select and list 12 derivatives and a word containing each derivative; for example:

audio	auditorium	*auto*	automatic
bios	biography	*civis*	civics
cyclos	bicycle	*deca*	decade
grapho	autograph	*mille*	millipede
centum	centipede	*octo*	octopus

Step 2:   One word from each pair is chosen and listed.

Step 3:   Players write the 12 words on the squares in their papers. Players choose where they put the words.

Step 4:   The remaining 12 words are called out and kept in the order in which they were read. As the words are called out, the players mark their papers. For example, if *decade* is called out, the players mark *deca*. The first player to complete a row calls out "Bingo!" and reads the words aloud.

Activities such as those described above provide students with opportunities to build their recognition and understanding of derivatives and how to use that knowledge when reading and writing.

Prefixes

Prefixes are words or parts of words that are placed in front of words to add to or change their meanings (Bolton & Snowball, 1993a). As with derivatives, prefixes are introduced after children have a core of known words and are beginning to understand the meaning relationships of words. It is not useful for students to memorize a long list of prefixes. Discussing prefixes, their meanings, and how they change the meanings of words are ways to introduce prefixes. Asking students to find prefixes in the materials they are reading will provide students with practice and understanding in how to apply knowledge of prefixes. The following list of prefixes, adapted from Bolton and Snowball (1993a), contains useful prefixes for primary grade learners.

Prefix	Meaning	Example
bi-	two	bicycle, bicep, binocular
dis-	not, do the opposite	display, disgrace, dispose
im-	not	impossible, immature
in-	into, within	include, income
pre-	before	preschool, prehistoric
re-	back, again	return, revisit, revise
step-	relationship due to remarriage	stepfather, stepmother
sub-	under, below, less than complete	submarine, subtract
super-	over, extra	superstar, superman
tri-	three	triangle, triplets, tripod
un-	not, reverse of	untie, unhealthy, unwise
under-	below	underground, underwear

Activities

During shared reading, the teacher and children can identify words with prefixes. These words can be listed on a class chart. For example, as Mrs. Quinn reads aloud *The Jolly Postman* (Janet and Allan Ahlberg, 1986), she writes the words with prefixes on a dry erase board. She and the students discuss the meaning of *bicycle* as "two wheels." They also discuss *displease*. Mrs. Quinn explains that *dis-* often means "not," so *displease* means "not to please or make happy." She also notes the words *stepmother* and *unexpected*. She asks the students to underline the prefix in each word. It is helpful to explain to the children that prefixes are always spelled the same way. This will help students to recognize the same prefix in different words. In order to practice recognizing prefixes, Mrs. Quinn asks her students to classify words with prefixes, putting all the words with the same prefix into one category. Mrs. Quinn and the students make prefix charts for their hanging rack of charts. The students continue to add words with prefixes throughout the school year.

Asking students to find words with prefixes in their independent reading material will also strengthen this skill. Children can use Post-its™ to write words with prefixes as they are reading. Some teachers use laminated bookmarks and dry erase markers for children to write words with prefixes; others use index cards. After writing these words, the children meet with the teacher to talk about the words, their prefixes, and on what charts they should be placed.

Working with the children, teachers can make a formula, such as the following, for words with prefixes.

Prefix	+	Base word	=	New word
un-		*happy*		*unhappy*

Ask children to make their own formula words and explain the meanings of the new words.

Children can also play card games like *Go Fish* with prefixes and base words. Activities such as these reinforce the students' learning about prefixes and will encourage them to recognize and use their knowledge of prefixes as they read and write.

Directions for Go Fish

Objective: Match as many pairs of cards as possible. A matched pair consists of a base word and the same word with a prefix.

Materials: Words and corresponding words with prefixes, such as *happy* and *unhappy*, written on cards.

Players: Any number

Prior to playing the game: Shuffle the cards and deal out five cards to each player. Place the remaining cards face down on the table. Hold cards so no one else can see them. Decide who will go first.

Playing the game: The first player asks another player for a matching card. For example, the first player has the card *happy* and says to the other player (Susie), "Do you have *unhappy?*"

If Susie has the card, she gives it to the first player. That player now has a match and places the pair of cards on the table in front of the player's place. That player takes another turn.

If Susie does not have a match, she says, "Go fish." The player who asked for the card takes one from the pile of cards on the table. If that card happens to be a match, the player puts the pair on the table and takes another turn. If the card is not a match, another player takes a turn.

The game continues until all the cards on the table are gone, and matches have been made from all the cards.
The player with the most matched pairs at the end of the game is the winner.

Suffixes

Suffixes come at the end of words. A suffix is a letter or word part added to the end of a word to make a new word. Suffixes give clues about the meaning of a word or the function of the speech. Suffixes can indicate what part of speech a word is. As with derivatives and prefixes, suffixes can be introduced when children have developed a core of known words and understand the meaning relationships between words. It is not useful for students to memorize a long list of suffixes. Introduce suffixes by discussing them and how they change the meanings of words. The meanings of many suffixes are somewhat abstract, and it is not necessary to spend a lot of time explaining meanings. As students reach third grade, teachers will want to discuss how a suffix can indicate what part of speech a word is. Asking students to find suffixes in the materials they are reading will provide students with practice in recognizing and understanding how to apply knowledge of suffixes. The following list of suffixes adapted from Bolton and Snowball (1993a) and *The Write Source* (1995) contains useful suffixes for primary grade learners.

Suffixes that denote nouns

-tion, -ation	nation, civilization, occupation
-er	teacher, baker, driver, racer
-ess	actress, goddess, lioness
-ness	kindness, emptiness

Suffixes that denote plurals

-s	cat/cats, dog/dogs, monkey, monkeys
-es	baby/babies, wish/wishes, tomato/tomatoes

Suffixes that denote adjectives

-al	natural, national
-ful	wonderful, beautiful
-less	careless, helpless, fearless

Suffixes that denote comparisons

-er (comparative)	longer, shorter, smaller
-est (superlative)	longest, shortest, smallest

Suffixes that denote verbs

-ate	cooperate, concentrate
-en	lighten, frighten

Suffixes that denote verb tense

-ed (past time)	looked, hunted
-ing (present time)	looking, hunting

Suffixes that denote adverbs

-ly	quickly, sadly
-ward	backward, forward

Activities

Finding suffixes during shared reading helps students to identify words with suffixes within text. Develop a class list with the students using words found during shared reading. While using the book *Good Morning, Who's Snoring?* (Mincherton, 1999), Mrs. Parker shows the students the *-ing* suffix in snoring. She then points out the *-ed* suffix in the words *barked, jumped, baaed, grunted,* and *shouted.* Mrs. Parker puts these words on a chart. *Snoring* is written on the chart containing other words with the *-ing* suffix, and she adds the *-ed* verbs to the chart on which she and the children have been collecting words ending with *-ed.* The students contribute other words with suffixes found in their independent reading materials. After discussing the words students find, the words are put on the charts or in class books. Students underline the suffixes. Words are sorted according to suffixes and placed in the book or on charts after sorting. These books and charts can serve as resources for the children to use when reading and writing. Cards with words containing suffixes can be placed in a center for the students to sort.

Students can also write the formula for suffixes as shown in the following example.

Base word	+	Suffix	=	New word
nation		*-al*		*national*
lion		*-ess*		*lioness*

Comparison charts can be made using the comparative and superlative forms of words. It is important to use base words that the students will be reading and wanting to use in their writing. Again, these charts can serve as resources for the children. The following is an example of a way to organize a comparison chart. For younger children, the headings may be omitted or simpler words can be sub-stituted as indicated in parenthesis.

Base word (word)	**Comparative** (next)	**Superlative** (most)
big	bigger	biggest
small	smaller	smallest
fast	faster	fastest
large	larger	largest
sweet	sweeter	sweetest
fat	fatter	fastest
happy	happier	happiest

Children will begin to notice that in some words the base word is changed when the suffix is added. It is then a good time to introduce some spelling gener-alizations about how words are changed. For example, when a word is a single syllable ending in a consonant and containing a short vowel, the final letter is doubled before adding the suffix, as in *big* and *fat*. Note that the suffix is always spelled the same; it is the base word that changes. Other useful generalizations are the following: When the word ends in *e*, the *e* is dropped before adding the suffix, as in *large*. When words end in *y*, the *y* is changed to *i* before adding the suffix, as in *happy*.

Teachers can introduce children to similar generalizations about adding *-s* and *-es* to form plurals. The teacher and students can generate a list of nouns, then the teacher invites children to make plurals. The teacher helps the children to demonstrate correctly spelled plurals. The students will notice that some base words don't change when you add *-s* and that others change when adding *-es*. They can state the generalization and find more plurals to fit the generalization, making class lists and charts for reference. Teachers or students can put base words and their corresponding plurals on cards for matching or memory games. For a matching game, the base word and plural can be written on the same card or sentence strip and cut to form a puzzle (Figure 8-1).

Memory Directions

Objective: To get the most matching cards

Players: Any number

Materials: Cards with base words and plurals written on them. The base words and their corresponding plurals are on separate cards.

To play the game: The cards are shuffled and placed face down on the playing surface. Players take turns turning the cards over, trying to

Figure 8-1. Matching Game

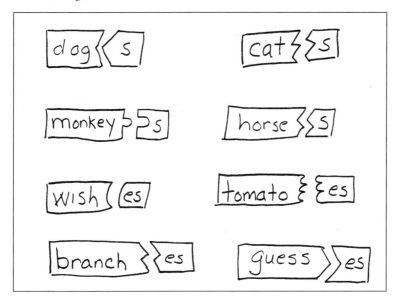

match base words and plurals. If a match is made, the player keeps both cards and gets another turn. If no match is made, the player turns the cards over again in the same location. Players try to remember where they saw cards so they can make matches. The game is over when all the cards have been matched. The winner is the player with the most pairs of cards.

Playing this game provides children with practice in automatically recognizing words and their plurals. This automaticity aids children in reading fluently and with comprehension.

Mrs. Irwin uses the book *Paul Bunyan* by Steven Kellogg (1984) to reinforce lessons about suffixes. The children find superlatives on the first page of the story, in addition to suffixes attached to verbs denoting past tense. The children find the words *business, wilderness,* and *meanness.* Mrs. Irwin and the children talk about how knowing the suffix *-ness* helped them read those words. Mrs. Irwin also asks another group of children to look for plurals in the book. Another group of children looks for words ending in *-ly* because Mrs. Irwin wants to demonstrate how adverbs work. She shows them how *heavily* and *neatly* make the verbs in the sentence more vivid and interesting. She encourages the children to use words with suffixes in their writing. Mrs. Irwin plans to reinforce this lesson with another of the children's favorite books, The *Z Was Zapped* by Chris Van Allsburg (1987). This is a book full of suffixes that makes extensive use of adverbs.

Activities such as those described here provide children with practice in recognizing and using suffixes. Easy recognition builds automaticity and fluency in reading. In addition, knowledge of suffixes can help children to determine unfamiliar words encountered in their reading. Students can also apply their knowledge of suffixes when writing to make their writing more interesting.

Compound Words

Compound words are words formed from two or more smaller words. The meaning of the compound word is related to the smaller words that make it, but a compound word is not just two or more words put together. Compound words are a bit more complex in that they differ somewhat in their underlying structure (Johnson & Pearson, 1984). For example, *birthday* is the day of one's birth; *moonlight* is the light from the moon; a *boxcar* is a car like a box; and a *tow truck* is a truck that tows. These differences can be explained to some grade 3 children who show an interest in the meanings of words, but for younger children it is probably enough for them to realize that compound words are made from more than one word. There are three kinds of compound words. They can be closed as in *breakfast*, open as in *truck driver*, or hyphenated as in *twenty-one*. It is not recommended that a list of compound words be memorized. Teachers can introduce compound words as soon as children have a core of known words.

Compound words are found in many books. They constitute many common vocabulary words. After reading the book *More Than Anything Else* (Bradby, 1995), Mrs. Atkins and her students return to the book to look for compound words. They compile a list: *anything, sunup, sundown, something, newspaper, everyone,* and *sometimes*. They talk about the meaning of the words, and the children notice that some of the parts of the words are used in more than one word. They begin to make other words, such as *someone, anyone,* and *anything*. Mrs. Atkins and her students put all the words into a class book of compound words.

Activities

Develop a list of words the children know in reading and writing or use one of the many published lists of commonly used words. Using one of these lists, teachers work with the children to make compound words. Older students may do this independently at a center or for homework. For example, how many compound words can be made using the following words?

any
every
one
thing
where
no
some
one
day
body

Teachers can ask students to find compound words in their reading materials. Using these words, class charts or books can be created. Students can work to define the compound words based on the smaller words, then check their definitions in the dictionary. Teachers or students can make lists of words to be combined into compound words (Figure 8-2). Students can generate the lists individually or in pairs and then ask other students to see how many compound words can be made from the list.

Figure 8-2. List for Compound Words

Sun	burn
break	down
any	up
every	one
Some	thing
no	body
tooth	where
birth	day
air	brush
	paste
	plane
	port
	line

Other activities include making a compound staircase (Bolton & Snowball, 1993a). A compound staircase is created by using the second part of a compound word as the first part of the next compound word. Figure 8-3 is an example of a compound word staircase.

Figure 8-3. Compound Word Staircase

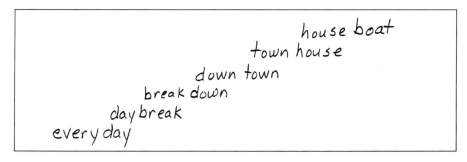

house boat
town house
down town
break down
day break
every day

Compound words can be used for the matching, Memory, and Bingo games described earlier in this chapter. Sorting compound words according to those with the same smaller words is another learning activity.

These activities provide students with meaningful practice with recognizing and writing compound words. Skill in recognizing compound words builds fluency and automaticity in reading. Knowing about compound words will assist readers in determining unfamiliar words encountered in reading.

Blended or Portmanteau Words

Blended words are words created by combining the first part of one word with the second part of another word. The meaning of the blended word comes from both the meanings of the words used to make it. Children can be introduced to blended words as soon as they have a core of known words and understand the meaning relationships of words. Children's oral language skills also need to be considered. Children need to be able to understand the words discussed and introduced.

Studying blended words also demonstrates the changing nature of language. The following list adapted from Bolton and Snowball (1993b) contains words familiar to primary students.

Blended Word	Sources
bit	binary digit
bookmobile	books + automobile
brunch	breakfast + lunch
chortle	chuckle + snort
moped	motor + pedal
motel	motor + hotel
newscast	news + broadcast
prissy	prim + sissy
sitcom	situation + comedy
smog	smoke + fog
telecast	television + broadcast
telethon	television + marathon
twiddle	twist/twirl + fiddle
twirl	twist + whirl

Activities

When introducing blended words, the teacher can talk about how language changes. Older students may think of examples of other words that show the addition of new words in our language. Teachers and students can make a class list of blended words and add to them as they discover new words. After learning about blended words, children can find them during both shared and independent reading. Blended words can also be used to play the matching games, Bingo, and Memory described in this chapter.

Contractions

Contractions are formed from two words. Letters are omitted, and those letters are represented by an apostrophe. Contractions are most frequently found in books containing dialogue because speech is less formal than written language and more contractions are used. Mrs. Smith chooses the book *Secret Soup* (Hessell, 1997) to point out contractions made from *is* and other words. In this book, *what's* and *it's* are repeated. Using magnetic letters, Mrs. Smith makes *what is* and shows the children how the *i* is omitted and an apostrophe is put in its place. She does the same with *it is*. The children practice reading the book with her, then independently. When reading *Noisy Nora* (Wells, 1973) aloud, Mrs. Smith asks the children to look for the *is* contractions. They find *she's* and *something's*. Mrs. Smith adds this to a class chart of *is* contractions. Mrs. Smith also uses *Noisy Nora* to point out the contraction *I'm*. She uses the magnetic letters again to demonstrate how *I* and *am* are put together. She starts a new chart.

Contractions can be sorted according to the second word embodied in the contraction. Here is a representative list adapted from Snowball and Bolton (1999). Students can generate their own list once they know and understand the categories.

am	is or has	are	will	not	have	had
I'm	it's	they're	I'll	can't	I've	I'd
	he's	we're	he'll	couldn't	they've	he'd
	here's	you're	she'll	didn't	we've	she'd
	she's		they'll	don't	you've	they'd
	there's			hadn't		we'd
	what's			hasn't		you'd
	who's			isn't		
				won't		

In addition to finding contractions during shared and independent reading, teachers can ask students to complete a contraction formula. In order to complete the formula, students must write a contraction and the words represented within it.

contraction	=	word	+	word
there's		*there*		*is*
we're		*we*		*are*
they'll		*they*		*will*
don't		*do*		*not*

Contractions can also be used to make matching, *Memory,* and *Bingo* games using the directions in this chapter. Encouraging students to include dialogue in their writing will also give them practice with applying knowledge of contractions in their writing.

Spelling

The study of morphemes and structural analysis of words contributes greatly to correct spelling. As students understand that suffixes and prefixes are consistently spelled the same way, they can use this knowledge in their writing. Developing an understanding of the generalizations governing the addition of suffixes will assist students as they spell words in their writing. Learning about structural analysis has a positive impact on students' use of correct, conventional spelling. Students who are exposed to direct instruction in structural analysis and have opportunities to engage in word play activities such as those described in this chapter notice words and attend to the correct letter sequence and the meaningful parts of the words. They use this knowledge to spell words when writing.

Assessment

Teachers can assess students' understanding of structural analysis in a number of ways. Examining student writing is one of the best ways to confirm what students know and need to learn about structural analysis. By looking at their students' writing, teachers determine what lessons in structural analysis need to be taught.

Figure 8-4. Interview Story

inter viewing a highpercondriac

We're here on Bailey's news interviewing Marianne Could you tell us what its like to be a high perconbriac? Well its like pretending to be sick.

Marianne why do you try if you know your going to get caught and in trouble? It's worth trying to do Something once, but I got a little carried away Do you ever feel like somebody else knows your not realy Sick?

yes because when my cheeks blush people know I am leing. Why did you decide to become a highper condriac? Because I want to get out of School. How do you feel now that your a retired highper con driac?

I feel better about myself.

Kemie, the first-grade child writing the interview story shown in Figure 8-4, demonstrates that she knows how to use *-ed* and *-ing* correctly; however, she does not properly apply the generalization that governs adding *-ing* to the word *lie.* She does properly change the *y* to *i* in *carry* before adding *-ed.* Kemie writes the compound word *something* correctly and uses the prefix *inter-* when writing *interviewing.* She probably recognizes and can spell the words *review, preview,* and *viewed* without difficulty. While correctly writing the contraction for *we're,* she does not consistently write *it's* correctly and incorrectly writes *you're.* Her temporary spelling of *hypochondriac* shows that she uses her knowledge of sounds and letters and applies what she knows about smaller words within words. Mrs. Parker first plans lessons to help Kemie better learn the contraction *it's* and then the contraction *you're.* These are frequently used words that she will need to use automatically as she writes. Mrs. Parker can then help her with the prefix *hypo-* to find the correct spelling of *hypochondriac,* but this word is not needed on a regular basis. Mrs. Parker may briefly discuss the differences between *hypo* and *hyper.* It is important that she help Kemie learn to spell automatically the words she will need most frequently in her writing, and then help her learn the tools for finding other words she wants to use in her writing.

Tanya's letter to her teacher (Figure 8-5) shows that she inconsistently applies her knowledge of using *-ed* correctly. Tanya is a second-grade student for whom English is not her first language. She demonstrates control over much of the language and spells many frequently used words correctly. Her teacher plans lessons to reinforce Tanya's use of *-ed.* Miss Fleischer points out *-ed* words in books and reviews when *-ed* is used.

Figure 8-5. Tanya's Letter

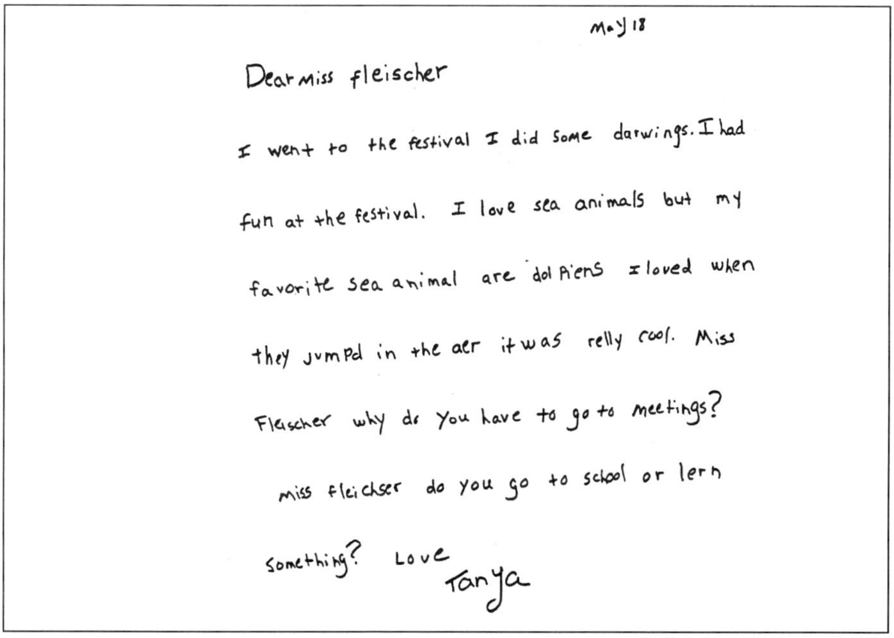
May 18

Dear miss fleischer

I went to the festival I did some darwings. I had fun at the festival. I love sea animals but my favorite sea animal are dolPiens I loved when they jumPd in the aer it was relly cool. Miss Fleischer why do You have to go to meetings? miss fleichser do you go to school or lern something? Love

Tanya

Figure 8-6. Virginia's Writing

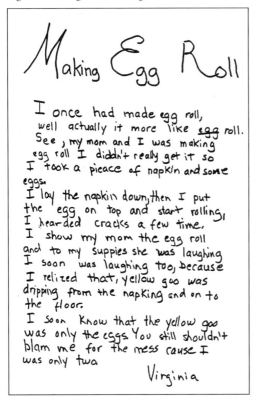

Making Egg Roll

I once had made egg roll,
well actually it more like egg roll.
See, my mom and I was making
egg roll I diddn't really get it so
I took a pieace of napkin and some
eggs.
I lay the napkin down, then I put
the egg on top and start rolling,
I hearded cracks a few time,
I show my mom the egg roll
and to my suppies she was laughing
I soon was laughing too, because
I relized that, yellow goo was
dripping from the napking and on to
the floor.
I soon know that the yellow goo
was only the eggs. You still shouldn't
blam me for the mess cause I
was only twa
                    Virginia

Virginia is a third-grade second language learner who shows she can spell many words correctly and use *-ing* correctly (Figure 8-6). She understands the generalizations applying to contractions, placing the apostrophe correctly in *didn't* and *shouldn't*. However, Virginia demonstrates inconsistent use of *-ed*. Mrs. Norton, her teacher, will review verb tenses with Virginia and ask her to find correct examples of verbs with *-ed* in her reading.

Although Virginia and Tanya are in different grades, they have similar needs. These girls demonstrate that instruction needs to be planned to meet the needs of children rather than follow a predetermined set of skills for a specific grade level. Teachers need to observe their students, listen to them read and talk, and examine their writing in order to know the instructional needs of each student.

Teachers can also assess students' understanding by asking them to do some of the matching or formula activities described in this chapter. Students who have trouble completing the activities may need extra lessons or more practice. For example, a student might have trouble matching prefixes or suffixes with base words to make a known word. Or a student might struggle to identify the words that are represented in contractions.

Listening to students read is another way to assess how well students apply knowledge of structural analysis. By listening for fluency and how students work on unknown words, the teacher can determine what each student knows about structural analysis. The teacher can note areas of strength and areas that need improvement.

Examining notes and anecdotal records based on the students' work in writing and reading, the teacher determines the needs of the students and groups them accordingly. The teacher reviews or reteaches specific lessons related to the demonstrated needs of the group. Once children demonstrate they have mastered these skills, the group is disbanded. The children in that group will meet with other groups needing specific lessons. Ongoing classroom assessment is the best way for teachers to ensure that students are successful in applying generalizations and developing skills in structural analysis.

APPENDIX A

Books That Promote
✳ Phonological Awareness ✳

Alliteration or Beginning Sounds

Base, G. (1986). *Animalia.* New York: Scholastic.

Bayer, J. (1984). *A, My Name Is Alice.* New York: Dutton.

Bender, R. (1996). *The A to Z Beastly Jamboree.* New York: Lodestar Books.

Brown, M. W. (1993). *Four Fur Feet.* NewYork: Doubleday.

Clements, A. (1997). *Double Trouble in Walla Walla.* Brookfield, CT: Millbrook Press.

Dragonwagon, C. (1992). *Alligator Arrived With Apples: A Potluck Alphabet Feast.* New York: Aladin Books.

Edwards, P. D. (1995). *Four Famished Foxes and Fosdyke.* New York: Harper Trophy.

Edwards, P. D. (1996). *Some Snug Slug.* New York: HarperCollins.

Edwards, P. D. (1997). *Dinorella: A Prehistoric Fairy Tale.* New York: Hyperion.

Gardner, B. (1986). *Have You Ever Seen…?* New York: Dodd, Mead.

Gordon, J. (1991). *Six Sleepy Sheep.* New York: Puffin.

Grover, M. (1993). *The Accidental Zucchini.* New York: Harcourt Brace.

Gustafson, S. (1994). *Alphabet Soup: A Feast of Letters.* Shelton, CT: Greenwich Workshop Press.

Hoberman, M. (1997). *Watch William Walk.* New York: Greenwillow.

Jahn-Clough, L. (1997). *ABC Yummy.* New York: Houghton Mifflin.

Kirk, D. (1998). *Miss Spider's ABC.* New York: Scholastic Press.

Merriam, E. (1989). *Where Is Everybody?* New York: Simon & Schuster.

Shelby, A. (1991). *Potluck.* New York: Orchard Books.

Yolen, J. (1990). *Elfabet: An ABC of Elves.* Boston: Little, Brown.

Rhymes

Alborough, J. (1998). *My Friend Bear.* Cambridge, MA: Candlewick Press.

Cameron, P. (1961). *"I Can't," Said the Ant.* New York: Scholastic.

Degen, B. (1990). *Jamberry.* New York: Scholastic.

Fox, M. (1998). *Boo to a Goose.* New York: Dial.

Fox, M. (1999). *Sleepy Bears.* New York: Harcourt Brace.

Guarino, D. (1989). *Is Your Mama a Llama?* New York: Scholastic.

Joyce, W. (1999). *Rolie Polie Olie.* New York: Harper Collins.

Koller, J. F. (1999). *Bouncing on the Bed.* New York: Orchard Books.

Lewison, W. (1992). *Buzz, Said the Bee.* New York: Scholastic.

Shaw, N. (1986). *Sheep in a Jeep.* Boston: Houghton Mifflin.

Shaw, N. (1989). *Sheep on a Ship.* Boston: Houghton Mifflin.

Shaw, N. (1991). *Sheep in a Shop.* Boston: Houghton Mifflin.

Shaw, N. (1992). *Sheep Out to Eat.* Boston: Houghton Mifflin.

Shaw, N. (1994). *Sheep Take a Hike.* Boston: Houghton Mifflin.

Waite J. (1998). *Mouse Look Out!* New York: Dutton.

Word Patterns

Cooper, M. (1998). *Pets!* New York: Holt.

Hawkins, C., & Hawkins, J. (1984). *Mig the Pig.* New York: Putnam.

Hawkins, C., & Hawkins, J. (1985). *Jen the Hen.* New York: Putnam.

Hawkins, C., & Hawkins, J. (1986). *Tog the Dog.* New York: Putnam.

Hawkins, C., & Hawkins, J. (1988). *Zug the Bug.* New York: Putnam.

Hawkins, C., & Hawkins, J. (1993). *Pat the Cat.* New York: Putnam.

Sound Manipulation

Buller, J., & Schade, S. (1988). *I Love You, Goodnight.* New York: Simon & Schuster.

Cowley, J. (1996). *Annabel.* Bothell, WA: Wright.

Falwell, C. (1998). *Word Wizards.* New York: Clarion Books.

Hutchins, P. (1976). *Don't Forget the Bacon.* New York: Greenwillow.

Plater, I. (1998). *Jolly Olly.* Crystal Lake, IL: Rigby.

Seuss, Dr. (1965). *Fox in Socks.* New York: Random House.

Slepian, J., & Seidler, A. (1999). *The Hungry Thing.* New York: Econo-Clad.

Wood, A. (1994). *Silly Sally.* New York: Harcourt Brace.

APPENDIX B

Alphabet Books

Simple Alphabet Books That Promote Naming the Letters

Bond, M. (1990). *Paddington's ABC.* New York: Puffin Books.

Cousins, L. (1994). *Maisy's ABC.* Cambridge, MA: Candlewick Press.

Crowther, R. (1999). *Robert Crowther's Most Amazing Hide and Seek Alphabet Book.* Cambridge, MA: Candlewick Press.

Eastman, P. D. (1974). *The Alphabet Book.* New York: Random House.

Gag, W. (1933). *The ABC Bunny.* New York: Putnam.

Geddes, A. (1995). *Anne Geddes ABC.* San Rafael, CA: Cedco.

Grover, M. (1993). *The Accidental Zucchini: An Unexpected Alphabet.* New York: Harcourt Brace.

Isadora, R. (1999). *ABC Pop.* New York: Penguin Putnam Books.

Johnson, A. (1989). *A to Z: Look and See.* New York: Random House.

Lobel, A. (1989). *On Market Street.* New York: Mulberry Books.

MacDonald, S. (1992). *Alphabetics.* New York: Aladdin.

Mayer, M. (1992). *Little Critter's ABC's.* New York: Random House.

McDonnell, F. (1997). *Flora McDonnell's ABC.* Cambridge, MA: Candlewick Press.

McPhail, D. (1989). *Animals A to Z.* New York: Scholastic.

Murphy, C. (1992). *My First Book of the Alphabet.* New York: Scholastic.

Nathan, C. (1995). *Bugs and Beasties ABC.* Boca Raton, FL: Cool Kids Press.

Wildsmith, B. (1962). *ABC.* Brookfield, CT: Millbrook Press.

Series of Alphabet Books

(One book for each letter; each page has a single illustration of an object beginning with that letter and the naming word for the object.)

The Alphabet Books. (1998). Greenvale, NY: Mondo.
Alphakids Alphabet Books. (1999). Littleton, MA: Sundance.
Phonics Readers Plus: The Alphabet Set. (1999). Austin, TX: Steck-Vaughn.
Markt, L. (1994). *Dominie Letter Books.* San Diego: Dominie Press.
Randell, B. (1996). *Alphabet Starters.* Crystal Lake, IL: Rigby.

Alphabet Books That Promote Letter-Sound Associations Through Alliteration

Base, G. (1986). *Animalia.* New York: Penguin.
Bayer, J. (1984). *A, My Name Is Alice.* New York: Dutton.
Bender, R. (1996). *The A to Z Beastly Jamboree.* New York: Lodestar Books.
Dragonwagon, C. (1992). *Alligator Arrived With Apples: A Potluck Alphabet Feast.*
    New York: Aladdin Books.
Gardner, B. (1986). *Have You Ever Seen…?* New York: Dodd, Mead.
Gustafson, S. (1994). *Alphabet Soup: A Feast of Letters.* Shelton, CT: Greenwich
    Workshop Press.
Jahn-Clough, L. (1997). *ABC Yummy.* New York: Houghton Mifflin.
Kirk, D. (1998). *Miss Spider's ABC.* New York: Scholastic Press.
Shelby, A. (1991). *Potluck.* New York: Orchard Books.
Yolen, J. (1990). *Elfabet: An ABC of Elves.* Boston: Little, Brown.

Alphabet Books That Promote Letter-Sound Associations Through Picture Hunts

Bourke, L. (1991). *Eye Spy: A Mysterious Alphabet.* San Francisco: Chronicle Books.
Demi. (1985). *Find the Animal's ABC.* New York: Grosset & Dunlap.
Kitanura, S. (1992). *From Acorn to Zoo and Everything in Between in Alphabetical
    Order.* New York: Farrar, Straus & Giroux.
Kitchen, B. (1984). *Animal Alphabet.* New York: Dial Books.
Rockwell, A. (1977). *Albert B. Cub & Zebra: An Alphabet Storybook.* New York:
    Harper & Row.
Rosenberg, L. (1997). *A Big and Little Alphabet.* New York: Orchard Books.
Sloat, T. (1989). *From Letter to Letter.* New York: Penguin Books.
Viorst, J. (1997). *The Alphabet From Z to A (With Much Confusion Along the Way).*
    New York: Aladdin.
Whatley, B., & Smith, R. (1994). *Whatley's Quest: An Alphabet Adventure.* New
    York: Harper Collins.

Alphabet Books That Promote Letter Identification Through Visual Details

Arnosky, J. (1999). *Mouse Letters: A Very First Alphabet Book.* New York: Clarion Books.
Tryon, L. (1991). *Albert's Alphabet.* New York: Aladdin.

Alphabet Books to Read Aloud

Aylesworth, J. (1992). *Old Black Fly.* New York: Holt.
Baker, A. (1994). *Black and White Rabbit's ABC.* New York: Larousse Kingfisher Chambers.
Duke, K. (1983). *The Guinea Pig ABC.* New York: Scholastic.
Edwards, P. (1999). *The Wacky Wedding: A Book of Alphabet Antics.* New York: Hyperion.
Ernst, L. C. (1996). *The Letters Are Lost.* New York: Puffin Books.
Greenfield, E. (1993). *Aaron and Gayla's Alphabet Book.* New York: Black Butterfly.
Lear, E. (1992). *A Was Once an Apple Pie.* New York: Scholastic.
Maurer, D. (1993). *Annie, Bea, and Chi Chi Dolores: A School Day Alphabet.* New York: Scholastic.
Merriam, D. (1989). *Where Is Everybody?* New York: Simon & Schuster.
Reasoner, C. (1998). *Alphabite! A Funny Feast From A to Z.* New York, NY: Price Stern Sloan.
Rey, H. A. (1963). *Curious George Learns the Alphabet.* Boston: Houghton Mifflin.
Slate, J. (1996). *Miss Bindergarten Gets Ready for Kindergarten.* New York: Scholastic.
Snow, A. (1991). *The Monster Book of ABC Sounds.* New York: Dial.

Alphabet Puzzle Books

Bruce, L. (1993). *Oliver's Alphabet.* New York: Bradbury Press.
Cahoon, H. (1999). *Word Play ABC.* New York: Walker.
Elting, M., & Folsom, M. (1980). *Q is for Duck: An Alphabet Guessing Game.* New York: Clarion Books.
Garten, J. (1994). *The Alphabet Tale.* New York: Greenwillow.
Joyce, Su. (1999). *ABC Animal Riddles.* Columbus, NC: Peel.
Kitamura, S. (1985). *What's Inside? The Alphabet Book.* New York: Farrar, Straus, & Giroux.
Shannon, G. (1996). *Tomorrow's Alphabet.* New York: Greenwillow.

Alphabet Concept Books

Books that develop understanding of a concept organized alphabetically

Aylesworth, J. (1992). *The Folks in the Valley.* New York: HarperCollins.

Demerest, C. (1999). *The Cowboy ABC.* New York: DK.

Ehlert, L. (1989). *Eating the Alphabet: Fruits and Vegetables From A to Z.* New York: Scholastic.

Feelings, M. (1974). *Jambo Means Hello: Swahili Alphabet Book.* New York: Dial Books.

Hepworth, C. (1992). *Antics.* New York: Putnam.

Jordan, M., & Jordan, T. (1996). *Amazon Alphabet.* New York: Scholastic.

Lobel, A. (1994). *Away From Home.* New York: Scholastic.

Onyefulu, I. (1993). *A is for Africa.* New York: Dutton.

Pallotta, J. (1996). *The Freshwater Alphabet Book.* New York: Charlesbridge.

REFERENCES

Adams, M. J. (1990). *Beginning to read: Thinking and learning about print.* Cambridge, MA: MIT Press.

Adams, M. J., Foorman, B. R., Lundberg, I., & Beeler, T. (1998). *Phonemic awareness in young children.* Baltimore, MD: Brookes.

Allington, R. L. (1997). Overselling phonics. *Reading Today, 15* (1), 15–16.

Anderson, R. C., Wilson, P. T., & Fielding, L. G. (1988). Growth in reading and how children spend their time outside school. *Reading Research Quarterly, 23,* 285–303.

Blachman, B. A. (1991). Early intervention for children's reading problems: Clinical applications of the research in phonological awareness. *Topics in Language Disorders, 12,* 51–65.

Bolton, F., & Snowball, D. (1993a). *Ideas for spelling.* Portsmouth, NH: Heinemann.

Bolton, F., & Snowball, D. (1993b). *Teaching spelling: A practical resource.* Portsmouth, NH: Heinemann.

Bond, G. L., & Dykstra, R. (1967). The cooperative research program in first-grade instruction. *Reading Research Quarterly, 2,* 1–142.

Bond, G. L., & Dykstra, R. (1997). The cooperative research program in first-grade instruction. *Reading Research Quarterly, 32,* 345–427.

Bradley, L., & Bryant, P. E. (1983). Categorizing sounds and learning to read: A causal connection. *Nature, 30,* 419–421.

Bradley, L., & Bryant, P. E. (1985). *Rhyme and reason in reading and spelling.* Ann Arbor, MI: University of Michigan Press.

Bredekamp, S. (1998). *Learning to read and write: Developmentally appropriate practices for young children.* Newark, DE: International Reading Association and National Association for the Education of Young Children.

Brown, H., & Cambourne, B. (1987). *Read and retell.* Portsmouth, NH: Heinemann.

Cambourne, B. (1988). *The whole story.* New York: Ashton Scholastic.

Carroll. J. B., Davies, P., & Richman, B. (1971). *Word frequency book.* Boston: Houghton Mifflin.

Catts, H. W. (1991). Early identification of reading disabilities. *Topics in Language Disorders 12* (1), 1–16.

Chaney, J. H. (1993). Alphabet books: Resources for learning. *The Reading Teacher, 47* (2), 96–104.

Chomsky, C. (1975). *The acquisition of syntax in children from 5 to 10.* Cambridge, MA: MIT Press.

Clay, M. M. (1991). Introducing a new storybook to young readers. *The Reading Teacher, 45,* 4, 264–273.

Clay, M. M. (1993a). *An observation survey of early literacy achievement.* Portsmouth, NH: Heinemann.

Clay, M. M. (1993b). *Reading recovery: A guidebook for teachers in training.* Portsmouth, NH: Heinemann.

Clymer, T. (1963). The utility of phonic generalizations in the primary grades. *The Reading Teacher, 16,* 252–258.

Cunningham, A., & Stanovich, K. (1998). What reading does for the mind. *American Educator, 22,* 8–15.

Cunningham, P. M. (1995). *Phonics they use: Words for reading and writing.* New York: HarperCollins.

Cunningham, P. M., & Hall, D. P. (1994). *Making words.* Torrance, CA: Good Apple.

Dyson, A. H. (1984). 'N spell my grandmamma: Fostering early thinking about print. *The Reading Teacher, 38,* 262–271.

Fege, P., Fowler, D., & Anzalone, B. (1998). *Sound teaching: A resource for teaching phonemic awareness and phonics instruction.* Fairfax, VA: Fairfax County Public Schools.

Ferreiro, E., & Teberosky, A. (1979). *Literacy before schooling.* Exeter, NH: Heinemann.

Fountas, I. C., & Pinnell, G. S. (1996). *Guided reading: Good first teaching for all children.* Portsmouth, NH: Heinemann.

Fowler, D., & McCallum, S. (1995a). *Primary purposes: Assessing.* Fairfax, VA: Fairfax County Public Schools.

Fowler, D., & McCallum, S. (1995b). *Primary purposes: Reading.* Fairfax, VA: Fairfax County Public Schools.

Fowler, D., & McCallum, S. (1995c). *Primary purposes: Writing.* Fairfax, VA: Fairfax County Public Schools.

Frith, U. (1985). Beneath the surface of developmental dyslexia. In K. Patterson, J. Marshall, & M. Coltheart (Eds.), *Surface dyslexia: Neuropsychological and cognitive studies of phonological reading* (pp. 301–330). London: Erlbaum.

Gentry, R. (1982). An analysis of developmental spelling in GNYS AT WRK. *The Reading Teacher, 36,* (2), 192–199.

Gibson, E. (1969). *Principles of perceptual learning and development.* New York: Prentice-Hall.

Goswami U., & Bryant, P. (1990). *Phonological skills and learning to read.* Hillsdale, NJ: Erlbaum.

Great Source Education Group, Inc. (1995). *The Write Source.* Wilmington, MA: Houghton-Mifflin.

Hall, N. (1987). *The emergence of literacy.* Portsmouth, NH: Heinemann.

Hayes, D. P., & Aherns, M. (1988). Vocabulary simplification for children: A special case for "motherease." *Journal of Memory and Language, 27,* 400–404.

Johnson, D. D., & Pearson, P. D. (1984). *Teaching reading vocabulary.* New York: Holt, Rinehart & Winston.

Juel, C. (1988). Learning to read and write: A longitudinal study of 54 children from first through fourth grades. *Journal of Educational Psychology, 80,* (4), 437–447.

Juel, C. (1991). Beginning reading. In R. Barr, M. L. Kamil, P. B. Mosenthal, & P. D. Pearson (Eds.), *Handbook of reading research, 2,* 759–788. Mahwah, NJ: Erlbaum.

Liberman, I. Y., Shankweiler, D., Fischer, F. W., & Carter, B. (1974). Explicit syllable and phoneme segmentation in the young child. *Journal of Experimental Child Psychology, 18,* 201–212.

Lie, A. (1991). Effects of a training program for stimulating skills in word analysis in first grade children. *Reading Research Quarterly 26,* 234–250.

Maclean, M., Bryant, P., & Bradley, L. (1987). Rhymes, nursery rhymes, and reading in early childhood. *Merrill-Palmer Quarterly, 33* (3), 255–281.

Mann, V. (1994). Phonological skills and the prediction of early reading problems. In N.C. Jordan, & J. Goldsmith-Phillips, (Eds.), *Learning disabilities: New directions for assessment and intervention.* Needham Heights, MA: Allyn & Bacon.

Mason, J. (1980). When do children begin to read: An exploration of four year old children's letter and word reading competencies. *Reading Research Quarterly, 15,* 203–227.

McCormick, C. E. & Mason, J. M. (1986). Intervention procedures for increasing preschool children's interest in and knowledge about reading. In W. H. Teale and E. Sulzby, (Eds.), *Emergent literacy: Writing and reading.* Norwood, NJ: Ablex.

McGee, L. M. & Richgels, D. J. (1989). K is Kristen's: Learning the alphabet from a child's perspective. *The Reading Teacher, 43,* 216–225.

Mooney, M. (1990). *Reading to, with, and by children.* Katonah, NY: Owen.

Morrow, L. M., Strickland, D., & Woo, D. G. (1998). *Literacy instruction in half- and whole-day kindergarten: Research to practice.* Newark, DE: International Reading Association.

Moustafa, M. H. (1997). *Beyond traditional phonics: Research discoveries and reading instruction.* Portsmouth, NH: Heinemann.

Perfetti, C. A., Beck, I., Bell, L., & Hughes, C. (1987). Phonemic knowledge and learning to read are reciprocal: A longitudinal study of first grade children. *Merrill-Palmer Quarterly, 33,* 283–319.

Pinnell, G. S., & Fountas, I. C. (1998). *Word matters: Teaching phonics and spelling in the reading/writing classroom.* Portsmouth, NH: Heinemann.

Pressley, M. (1998). *Reading instruction that works: The case for balanced teaching.* New York: Guilford Press.

Read, C. (1971). Pre-school children's knowledge of English phonology. *Harvard Educational Review, 41,* 1–34.

Smolkin, L., & Yaden, D. (1992). O is for mouse: First encounters with the alphabet book. *Language Arts, 69,* 432–441.

Snow, C., Burns, M. S., & Griffith, P. (Eds.) (1998). *Preventing reading difficulties in young children.* Washington, DC: National Academy Press.

Snowball, D., & Bolton, F. *Spelling K–8: Planning and teaching.* York, ME: Stenhouse.

Stanovich, K. E. (1986). Matthew effects in reading: Some consequences of individual differences in the acquisition of literacy. *Reading Research Quarterly, 21,* 360–407.

Stanovich, K. E., Cunningham, A. E., & Cramer, B. B. (1984). Assessing phonological awareness in kindergarten children: Issues of task comparability. *Journal of Experimental Child Psychology, 3* (2), 175–190.

Strickland, D. S. (1998). *Teaching phonics today.* Newark, DE: International Reading Association.

Treiman, R. (1986). The division between onsets and rimes in English syllables. *Journal of Memory and Language, 25,* 476–491.

Treiman, R., & Baron, J. (1981). Segmental analysis ability: Development and relation to reading ability. In G. E. McKinnon & T. G. Waller (Eds.), *Reading research: Advances in theory and practice* (Vol. 3). New York: Academic Press.

Treiman, R., & Chafetz, J. (1987). Are there onset-and rime-like units in printed words? In M. Colehart (Ed.), *Attention and performance 12: The psychology of reading.* Hillsdale, NJ: Erlbaum.

Vernon, S., & Ferreiro, E. (1999). Writing development: A neglected variable in the consideration of phonological awareness. *Harvard Educational Review, 69,* 395–415.

Vygotsky, L. S. (1962). In E. Haufman & G. Vakas (Eds. and Trans.), *Thought and language.* Cambridge, MA: MIT Press.

Wagner, R. K., Torgesen, J. K., & Raschotte, C. A. (1994). Development of reading-related phonological processing abilities: New evidence of bidirectional causality from a latent variable longitudinal study. *Developmental Psychology, 30* (1), 73–87.

Wagstaff, J. (1994). *Phonics that work!* New York: Scholastic.

Wilde, S. (1997). *What's a schwa sound anyway?: A holistic guide to phonetics, phonics, and spelling.* Portsmouth, NH: Heinemann.

Winner, H., Landerl, K., Linortner, R., & Hummer, P. (1991). The relationship of phonemic awareness to reading acquisition: More than precondition but still important. *Cognition, 40,* 219–249.

Yopp, H. K. (1988). The validity and reliability of phonemic awareness tests. *Reading Research Quarterly, 23,* 159–177.

Yopp, H. K., & Yopp, R. H. (1997). *Oo-pples and boo-noo-noos: Songs and activities for phonemic awareness.* New York: Harcourt Brace.

Children's Books

Ahlberg, J., & Ahlberg. A. (1986). *The jolly postman.* Boston: Little, Brown.

Barchas, S. (1993). *I was walking down the road.* New York: Scholastic.

Barton, B. (1989). *Dinosaurs, Dinosaurs.* New York: HarperCollins.

Bayer, J. (1984). *A, My name is Alice.* New York: Dutton.

Bender, R. (1996). *The A to Z beastly jamboree.* New York: Lodestar Books.

Bradby, M.(1995). *More than anything else.* New York: Orchard Books.

Brown, M. (1987). *Play rhymes.* New York: Scholastic.

Cameron, P. (1961).*"I can't," said the ant.* New York: Scholastic.

Carle, E. (1971). *Do you want to be my friend?* New York: Crowell.

Carle. E. (1991). *Have you seen my cat?* New York: Scholastic.

Climo, S. (1989). *The Egyptian Cinderella.* New York. Crowell.

Cowley, J. (1983). *The meanies.* Bothell, WA: Wright.

Cowley, J. (1990a). *The farm concert.* Bothell, WA: Wright.

Cowley, J. (1990b). *Mrs. Wishy-washy.* Bothell, WA: Wright.

Cowley, J. (1990c). *Who Will Be My Mother?* Bothell, WA:Wright.

Cowley, J. (1991). *Greedy cat.* Wellington, New Zealand: Ministry of Education.

Degen, B. (1990). *Jamberry.* New York: Scholastic.

Ernst, L. (1996). *The letters are lost.* New York: Puffin.

Guarino, D. (1991). *Is your mama a llama?* New York: Scholastic.

Gustafson, S. (1994). *Alphabet soup: A feast of letters.* Shelton, CT: Greenwich Workshop Press.

Hessell, J. (1997). *Secret soup.* Crystal Lake, IL: Rigby.

Hill, E. (1980). *Where's Spot?* New York: Putnam.

Hoban, T. (1984). *I walk and read.* New York: Greenwillow.

Hoban, T. (1987). *I read signs.* New York: Morrow.

Hoban, T. (1988). *I read symbols.* New York: Morrow.

Hutchins, P. (1983). *Rosie's walk.* New York: Aladdin

Hutchins, P. (1989). *Don't forget the bacon.* New York: Mulberry Books.

Jordan, M., & Jordan, T. (1996). *Amazon alphabet.* New York: Scholastic.

Kellogg, S. (1984). *Paul Bunyan.* New York: Morrow.

Kline, S. (1998). *Horrible Harry and the dungeon.* New York: Puffin.

Lewison, W. (1992). *"Buzz," said the bee.* New York: Scholastic.

Loredo, E. (1996). *The jump rope book.* New York: Workman.

MacDonald, S. (1992). *Alphabetics.* New York: Aladdin.

Martin, B., Jr., (1967). *Brown bear, brown bear, what do you see?* New York: Holt.

McDaniel, B. B. (1983). *Katie did it.* New York: Children's Press.

McLeod, E. (1975). *The bear's bicycle.* Boston: Little, Brown.

McPhail, D. (1989). *Animals A to Z.* New York: Scholastic.

Mincherton, A. (1999). *Good morning, who's snoring?* Crystal Lake, IL: Rigby.

Park, B. (1987). *The kid in the red jacket.* New York: Random House.

Pilkey, D. (1994). *A friend for dragon.* New York: Orchard.

Polacco, P. (1996). *Aunt Chip and the great triple creek dam affair.* New York: Philomel Books.

Randell, B. (1994). *Kitty and the Birds.* Crystal Lake, IL: Rigby.

Rylant, C. (1985). *The relatives came.* New York: Aladdin.

Scamell, R. (1992). *Solo plus one.* Boston: Little, Brown.

Semple, C., & Tuer, J. (1997). *Just like grandpa.* Crystal Lake, IL: Rigby.

Seuss, Dr. (1965). *Hop on pop.* New York: Random House.

Shannon, G. (1996). *Tomorrow's alphabet.* New York: Greenwillow.

Shaw, N. (1989). *Sheep on a ship.* Boston: Houghton Mifflin

Sloat, T. (1989). *From letter to letter.* New York: Penguin Books.

Smith, R. (1998). *Spring snow.* Orono, ME: University of Maine Center for Early Literacy.

Snow, A. (1991). *The monster book of ABC sounds.* New York: Dial Books.

Speed, T. (1995). *Two cool cows.* New York: Scholastic.

Tafuri, N. (1984). *Have you seen my duckling?* New York: Greenwillow.

Tryon, L. (1991). *Albert's alphabet.* New York: Aladdin Paperbacks.

Van Allsburg, C., (1987). *The Z was zapped.* Boston: Houghton Mifflin.

Vaughan, M. (1997). *Moonlight.* Crystal Lake, IL: Rigby.

Wells, R. (1973). *Noisy Nora.* New York: Scholastic.

Wildsmith, B. (1982). *Cat on the mat.* Oxford, England: OxfordUniversity Press.

Williams, S. (1990). *I went walking.* San Diego: Harcourt Brace.

INDEX

Jean R. Frey currently works for the Fairfax County (VA) Public Schools as the Coordinator for Elementary Standards of Learning and Remediation. Prior to that she worked as a language arts specialist; an elementary school-based reading teacher trained in Reading Recovery; and classroom teacher of grades 1, 3, and 4. She has been actively involved in teacher research exploring the topics of beginning reading, writing conferences, vocabulary development, and the teacher research process. In her present position, Jean is interested in standards-based learning and school reform.

Dorothy J. Fowler is a primary language arts specialist with the National Center on Education and the Economy. She was a member of the National Research Council Committee that produced the report *Preventing Reading Difficulties in Young Children.* Her professional experiences have included work as a primary classroom teacher, Reading Recovery teacher, clinical supervisor, language arts curriculum teacher, and early childhood specialist. She has written articles for *Educational Leadership* and is the author of the facilitator's guide for the ASCD video series *The Brain and Reading.* Her current work focuses on literacy development in the context of standards-based school reform.